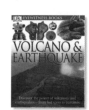

Eyewitness
SKELETON

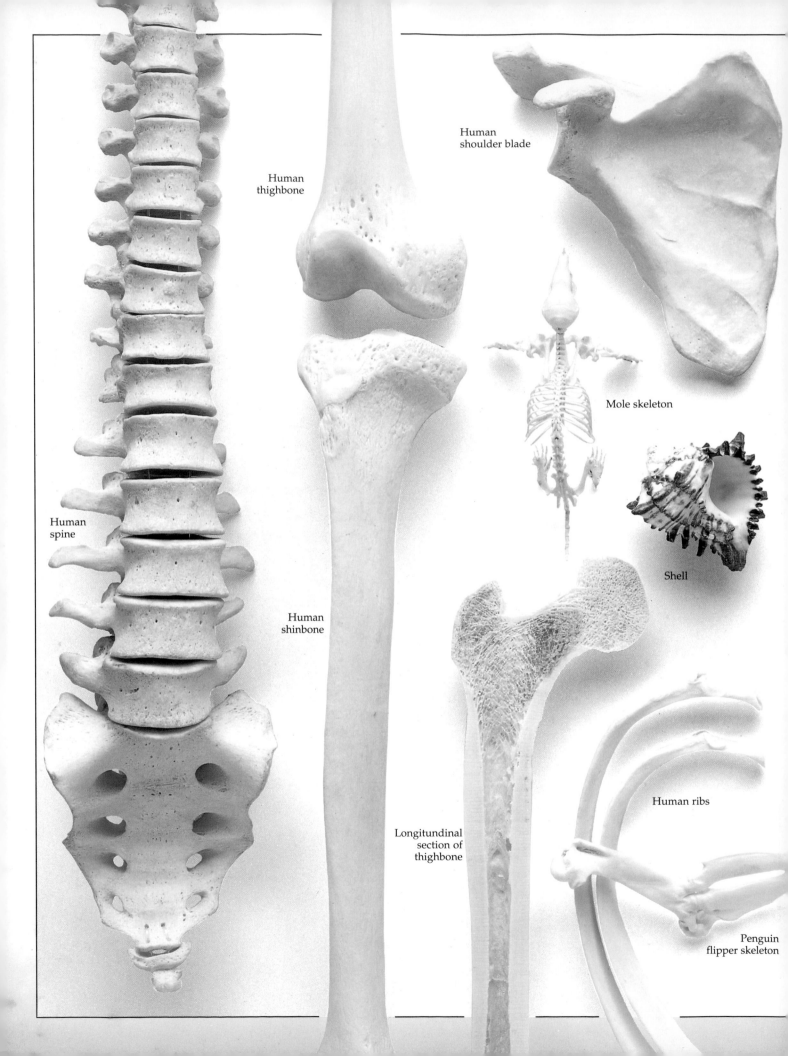

Human thighbone

Human shoulder blade

Human spine

Human shinbone

Mole skeleton

Shell

Longitundinal section of thighbone

Human ribs

Penguin flipper skeleton

Human
molars

Star shell

Eyewitness
SKELETON

Written by
STEVE PARKER

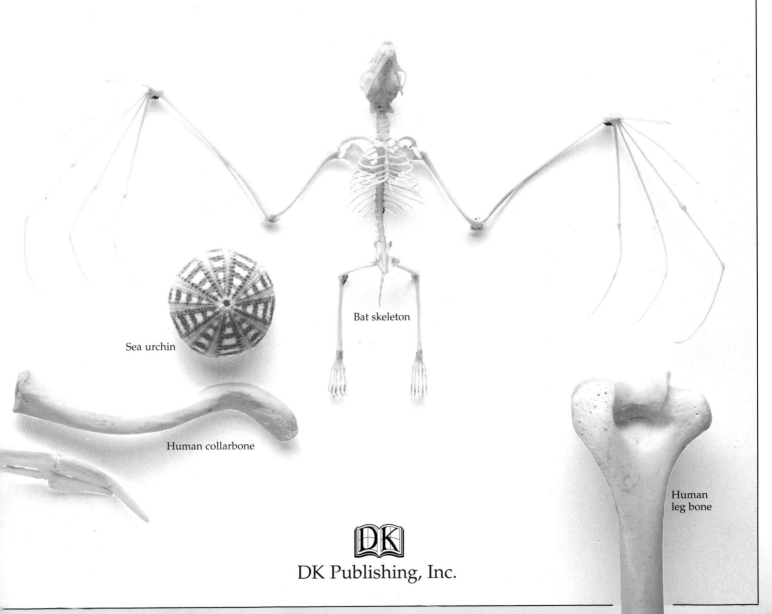

Sea urchin

Bat skeleton

Human collarbone

Human
leg bone

DK

DK Publishing, Inc.

Fox skull

Lizard skeleton

Cuttlebone

Scallop shell

LONDON, NEW YORK, MELBOURNE,
MUNICH, and DELHI

Project editor Sophie Mitchell
Managing art editor Jane Owen
Assistant designer Martyn Foote
Special photography Philip Dowell
Editorial consultants
The staff of The Natural History Museum, London

REVISED EDITION
Managing editor Andrew Macintyre
Managing art editor Jane Thomas
Editor and reference compiler Mary Atkinson
Art editor Chris Fraser
Production Jenny Jacoby
Picture research Sarah Pownall
DTP designer Siu Ho

U.S. editor Elizabeth Hester
Senior editor Beth Sutinis
Art director Dirk Kaufman
U.S. production Chris Avgherinos
U.S. DTP designer Milos Orlovic

This Eyewitness ® Guide has been conceived by
Dorling Kindersley Limited and Editions Gallimard

This edition published in the United States in 2004
by DK Publishing, Inc., 375 Hudson Street, New York, New York 10014

07 08 10 9 8 7 6 5 4 3

A catalog record for this book is
available from the Library of Congress.

ISBN 978-0-7566-0727-2 (PLC) 978-0-7566-0726-5 (ALB)

Color reproduction by Colourscan, Singapore
Printed in China by Toppan Printing Co. (Shenzhen), Ltd.

Discover more at
www.dk.com

Human
rib

Human
forearm bone

Whelk shell

Bird-wing
skeleton

Contents

Crow skull

Parrot skull

The human skeleton

A SKELETON IS MANY THINGS: symbol of danger and death, a key that opens any door, a secret kept in a closet, the outline of a novel or grand plan . . . and the 200-odd bones that hold up each human body. Our skeleton supports, moves and protects. It is both rigid and flexible. Individual bones are stiff and unyielding, forming an internal framework that supports the rest of the body and stops it collapsing into a jelly-like heap. Bones together, linked by movable joints and worked by muscles, form a system of girders, levers and pincers that can pick pick an apple from a tree or move the body forward at 20 mph (32 kph). The skeleton protects our most delicate and important organs: the skull shields the brain, and the ribs guard the heart and lungs. The human skeleton follows the basic design found in the 40,000 or so species of backboned animals. But the endless variety of animals has a correspondingly endless variety of skeletons, as this book sets out to show.

BIG HEAD
In relation to body size, the human skull houses one of the biggest brains in the animal world (p. 26).

EARLY IMPRESSION *above*
Medical textbooks of the 18th and 19th centuries would have contained detailed illustrations such as this.

ANATOMY LECTURE *below*
A medieval lecture theater populated by human and animal skeletons.

MEDIEVAL MEDICINE
The surgeon points out details of the rib cage to a 15th-century student.

FOOD PROCESSORS
Human teeth chop their way through about 500 kg (half a ton) of food each year (p. 27).

MEASURING THE SKULL
The craniometer, a device for measuring skull size - and, by deduction, brain size.

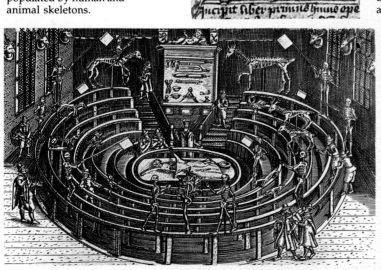

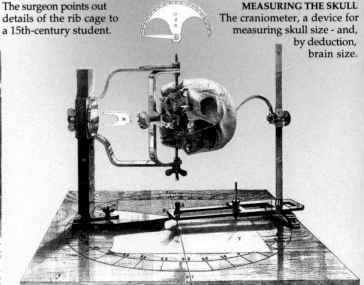

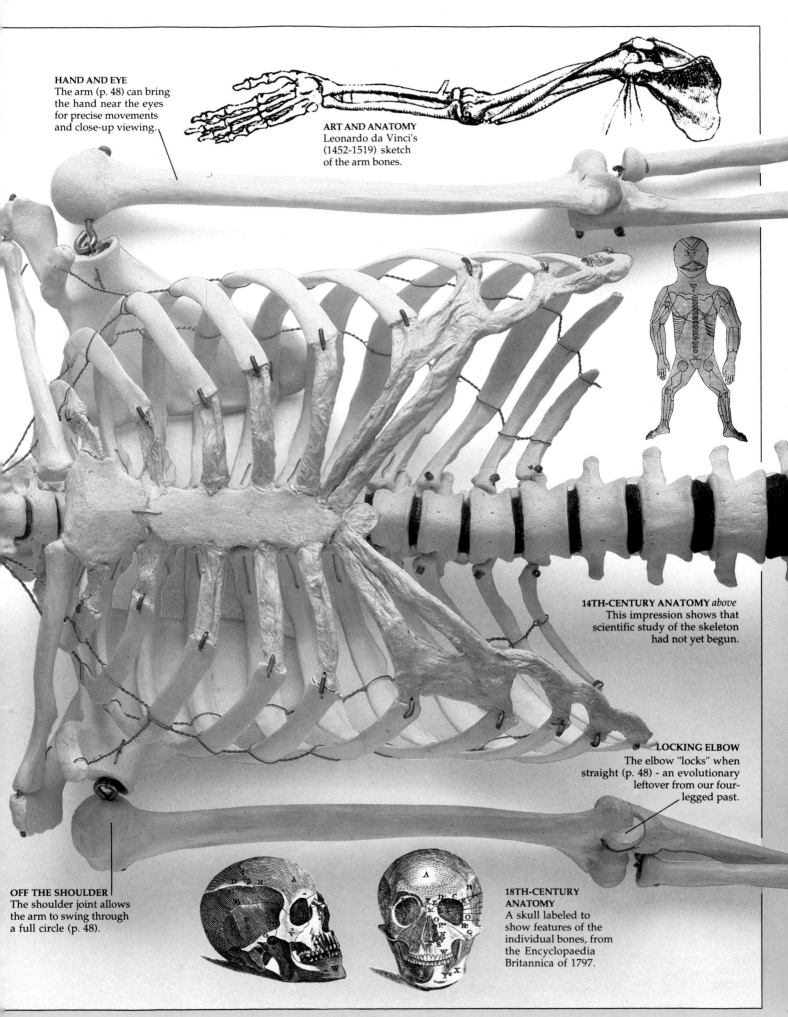

HAND AND EYE
The arm (p. 48) can bring the hand near the eyes for precise movements and close-up viewing.

ART AND ANATOMY
Leonardo da Vinci's (1452-1519) sketch of the arm bones.

14TH-CENTURY ANATOMY *above*
This impression shows that scientific study of the skeleton had not yet begun.

LOCKING ELBOW
The elbow "locks" when straight (p. 48) - an evolutionary leftover from our four-legged past.

OFF THE SHOULDER
The shoulder joint allows the arm to swing through a full circle (p. 48).

18TH-CENTURY ANATOMY
A skull labeled to show features of the individual bones, from the Encyclopaedia Britannica of 1797.

7

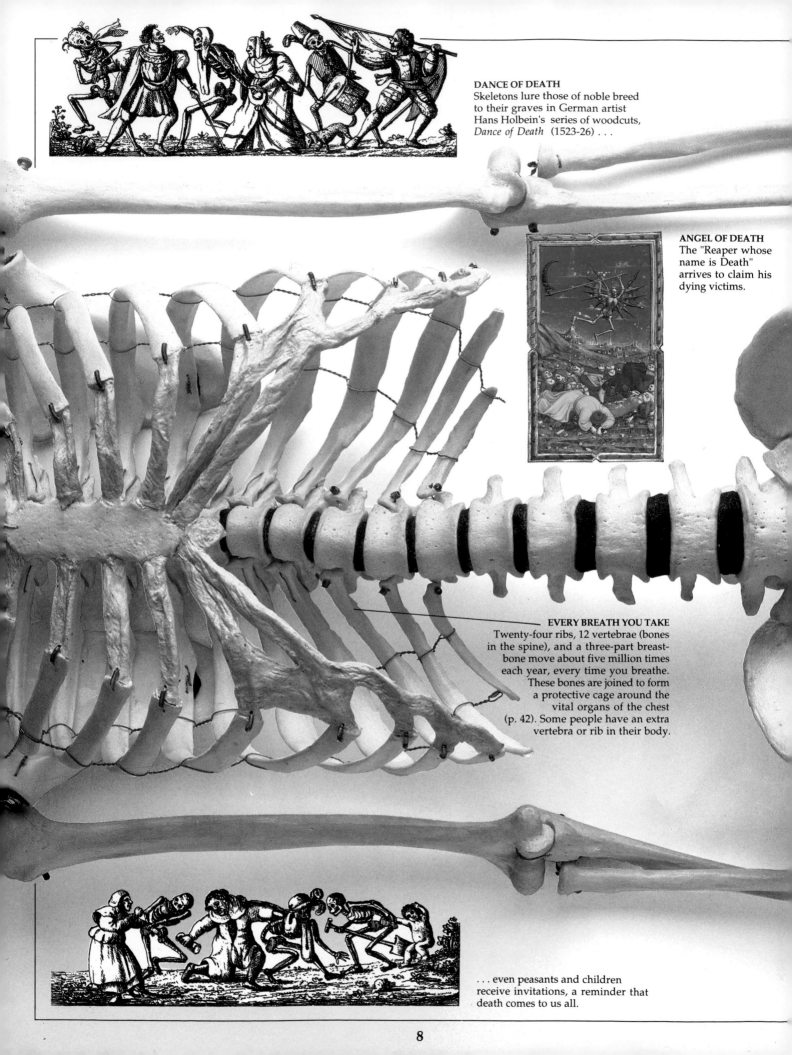

DANCE OF DEATH
Skeletons lure those of noble breed to their graves in German artist Hans Holbein's series of woodcuts, *Dance of Death* (1523-26) . . .

ANGEL OF DEATH
The "Reaper whose name is Death" arrives to claim his dying victims.

EVERY BREATH YOU TAKE
Twenty-four ribs, 12 vertebrae (bones in the spine), and a three-part breast-bone move about five million times each year, every time you breathe. These bones are joined to form a protective cage around the vital organs of the chest (p. 42). Some people have an extra vertebra or rib in their body.

. . . even peasants and children receive invitations, a reminder that death comes to us all.

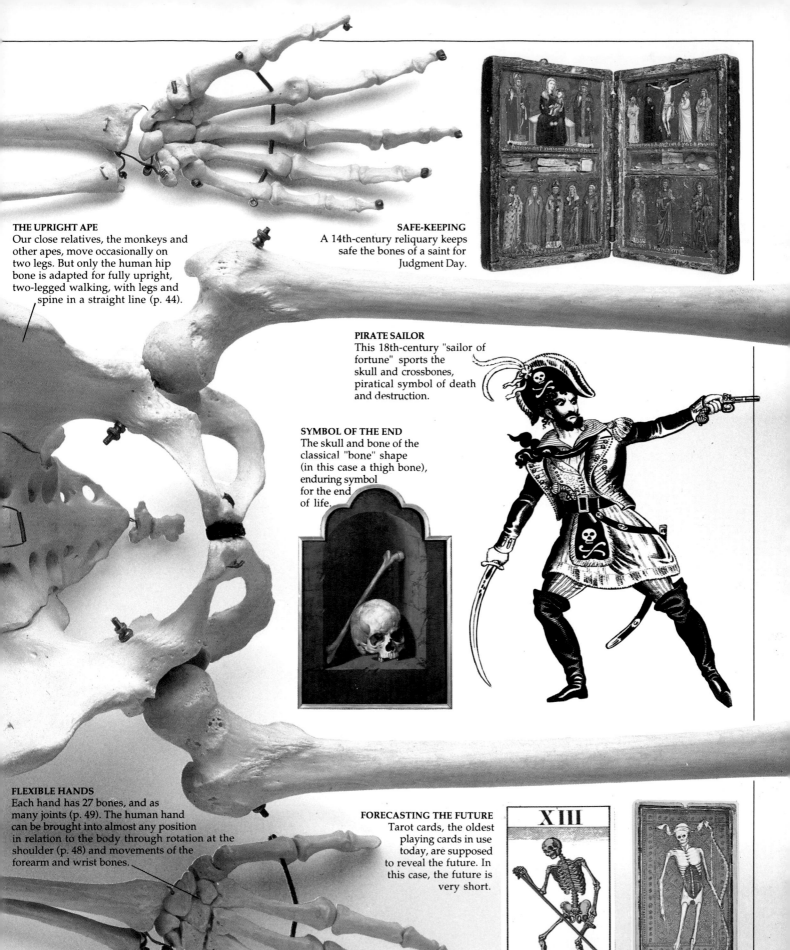

THE UPRIGHT APE
Our close relatives, the monkeys and other apes, move occasionally on two legs. But only the human hip bone is adapted for fully upright, two-legged walking, with legs and spine in a straight line (p. 44).

SAFE-KEEPING
A 14th-century reliquary keeps safe the bones of a saint for Judgment Day.

PIRATE SAILOR
This 18th-century "sailor of fortune" sports the skull and crossbones, piratical symbol of death and destruction.

SYMBOL OF THE END
The skull and bone of the classical "bone" shape (in this case a thigh bone), enduring symbol for the end of life.

FLEXIBLE HANDS
Each hand has 27 bones, and as many joints (p. 49). The human hand can be brought into almost any position in relation to the body through rotation at the shoulder (p. 48) and movements of the forearm and wrist bones.

FORECASTING THE FUTURE
Tarot cards, the oldest playing cards in use today, are supposed to reveal the future. In this case, the future is very short.

XIII

LA MORT

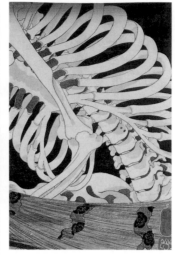

EASTERN MAGIC
Mitsukuni, a Japanese sorceress, summons up a giant skeleton to frighten her enemies in this painting by Kuniyoshi.

THE LONGEST BONES
The bones in the leg are the longest in the human body (p. 54). The leg bones are shaped to allow their lower ends - at the ankles and knees - to touch, while the tops of the thigh bones - at the hip - may be more than 1 ft (30 cm) apart.

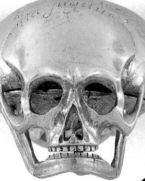

MARKING TIME *left*
The seconds tick by for this silver skull - it is the case for a watch, made in Germany in about 1620.

Detail of distorted skull shown in the painting on the right

ARTIST'S ILLUSION
Hans Holbein's *The Ambassadors* (1533) records the opulence of Henry VIII's court;

the odd shape in the foreground is a distorted skull, seen more clearly from one side and very close. (The name Holbein can be translated as "hollow bone".)

THE LOCKING KNEE
The knee is the largest joint in the body (p. 54), carrying as it does almost half the body's weight. It forms a locking hinge that bends in one direction only.

ALAS, POOR YORICK . . .
Shakespeare's Hamlet (portrayed by a French actor) ponders the skull of the Danish court jester Yorick: "That skull had a tongue in it, and could sing once . . ."

SKULL CUP
The holy lamas (priests) of Tibet use ceremonial cups like this, made from the top of a human skull, symbol of consuming the mind of another.

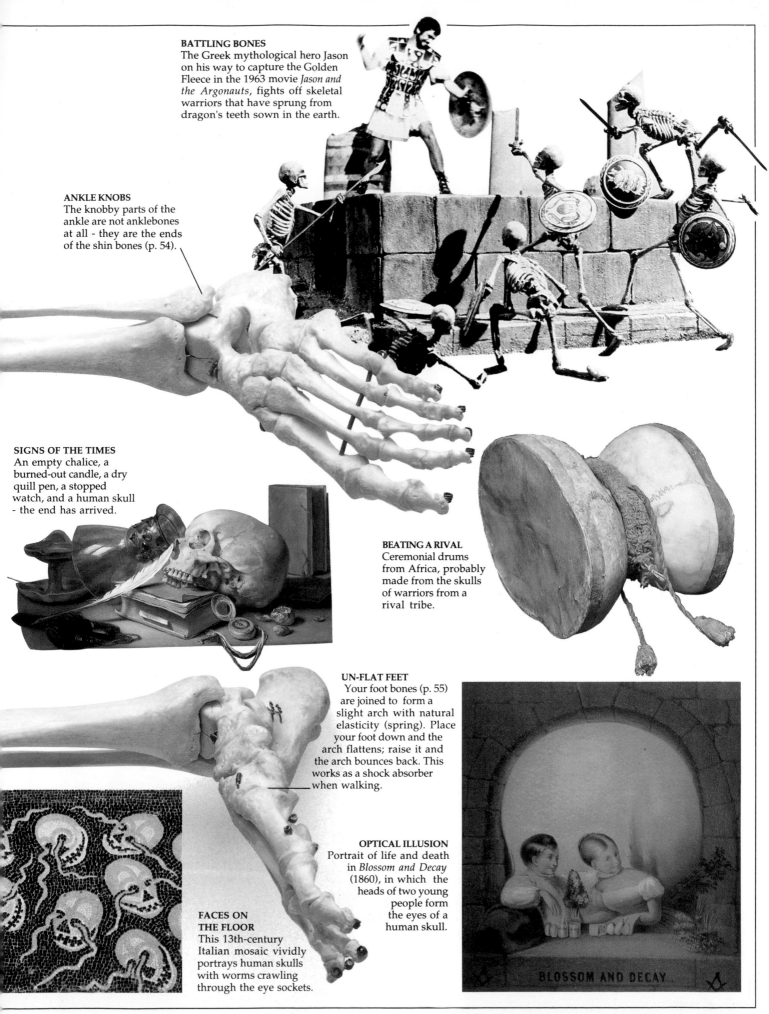

BATTLING BONES
The Greek mythological hero Jason on his way to capture the Golden Fleece in the 1963 movie *Jason and the Argonauts*, fights off skeletal warriors that have sprung from dragon's teeth sown in the earth.

ANKLE KNOBS
The knobby parts of the ankle are not anklebones at all - they are the ends of the shin bones (p. 54).

SIGNS OF THE TIMES
An empty chalice, a burned-out candle, a dry quill pen, a stopped watch, and a human skull - the end has arrived.

BEATING A RIVAL
Ceremonial drums from Africa, probably made from the skulls of warriors from a rival tribe.

UN-FLAT FEET
Your foot bones (p. 55) are joined to form a slight arch with natural elasticity (spring). Place your foot down and the arch flattens; raise it and the arch bounces back. This works as a shock absorber when walking.

OPTICAL ILLUSION
Portrait of life and death in *Blossom and Decay* (1860), in which the heads of two young people form the eyes of a human skull.

FACES ON THE FLOOR
This 13th-century Italian mosaic vividly portrays human skulls with worms crawling through the eye sockets.

BLOSSOM AND DECAY

From bone to stone

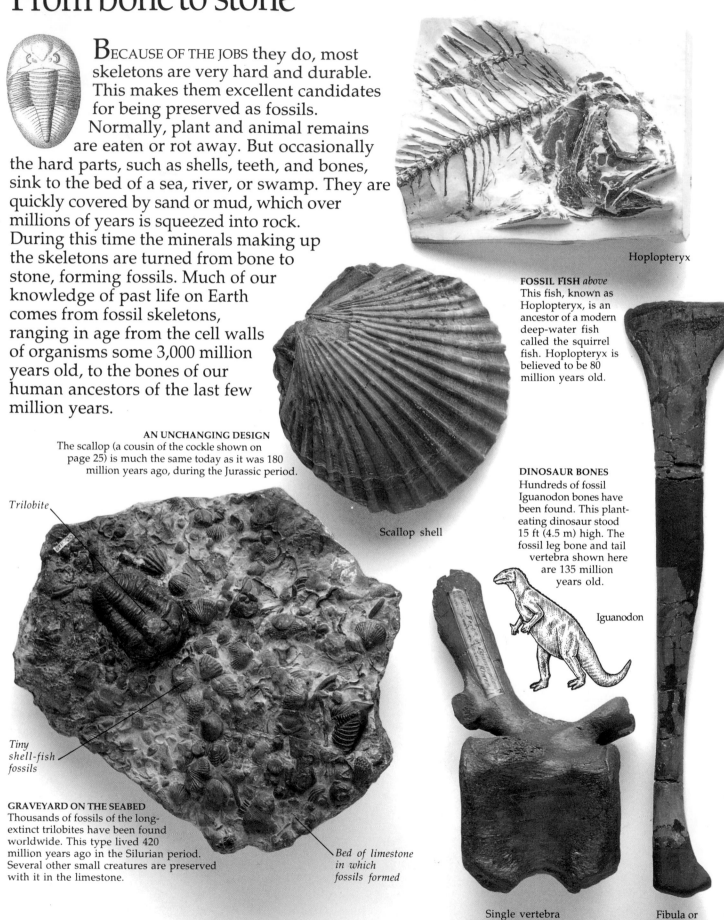

BECAUSE OF THE JOBS they do, most skeletons are very hard and durable. This makes them excellent candidates for being preserved as fossils. Normally, plant and animal remains are eaten or rot away. But occasionally the hard parts, such as shells, teeth, and bones, sink to the bed of a sea, river, or swamp. They are quickly covered by sand or mud, which over millions of years is squeezed into rock. During this time the minerals making up the skeletons are turned from bone to stone, forming fossils. Much of our knowledge of past life on Earth comes from fossil skeletons, ranging in age from the cell walls of organisms some 3,000 million years old, to the bones of our human ancestors of the last few million years.

Hoplopteryx

FOSSIL FISH *above*
This fish, known as Hoplopteryx, is an ancestor of a modern deep-water fish called the squirrel fish. Hoplopteryx is believed to be 80 million years old.

AN UNCHANGING DESIGN
The scallop (a cousin of the cockle shown on page 25) is much the same today as it was 180 million years ago, during the Jurassic period.

Scallop shell

DINOSAUR BONES
Hundreds of fossil Iguanodon bones have been found. This plant-eating dinosaur stood 15 ft (4.5 m) high. The fossil leg bone and tail vertebra shown here are 135 million years old.

Iguanodon

Trilobite

Tiny shell-fish fossils

GRAVEYARD ON THE SEABED
Thousands of fossils of the long-extinct trilobites have been found worldwide. This type lived 420 million years ago in the Silurian period. Several other small creatures are preserved with it in the limestone.

Bed of limestone in which fossils formed

Single vertebra from the dinosaur's tail

Fibula or lower leg bone

Complete Ichthyosaur
skeleton

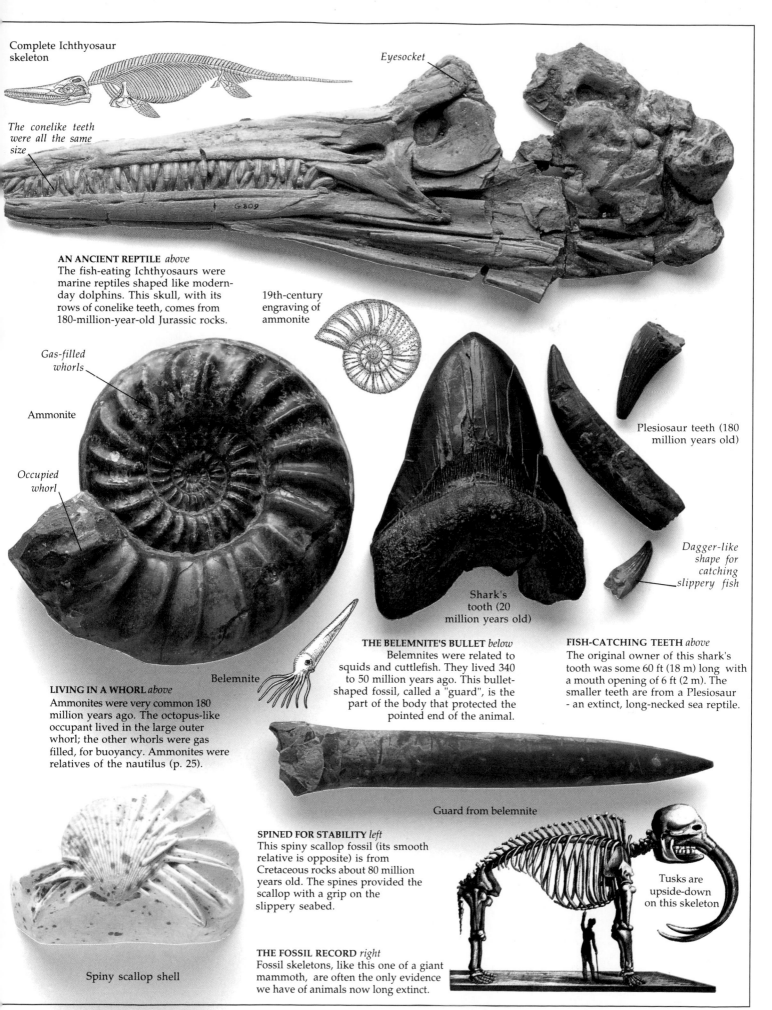

Eyesocket

*The conelike teeth
were all the same
size*

G 809

AN ANCIENT REPTILE *above*
The fish-eating Ichthyosaurs were
marine reptiles shaped like modern-
day dolphins. This skull, with its
rows of conelike teeth, comes from
180-million-year-old Jurassic rocks.

19th-century
engraving of
ammonite

*Gas-filled
whorls*

Ammonite

*Occupied
whorl*

Plesiosaur teeth (180
million years old)

*Dagger-like
shape for
catching
slippery fish*

Shark's
tooth (20
million years old)

FISH-CATCHING TEETH *above*
The original owner of this shark's
tooth was some 60 ft (18 m) long with
a mouth opening of 6 ft (2 m). The
smaller teeth are from a Plesiosaur
- an extinct, long-necked sea reptile.

Belemnite

THE BELEMNITE'S BULLET *below*
Belemnites were related to
squids and cuttlefish. They lived 340
to 50 million years ago. This bullet-
shaped fossil, called a "guard", is the
part of the body that protected the
pointed end of the animal.

LIVING IN A WHORL *above*
Ammonites were very common 180
million years ago. The octopus-like
occupant lived in the large outer
whorl; the other whorls were gas
filled, for buoyancy. Ammonites were
relatives of the nautilus (p. 25).

Guard from belemnite

SPINED FOR STABILITY *left*
This spiny scallop fossil (its smooth
relative is opposite) is from
Cretaceous rocks about 80 million
years old. The spines provided the
scallop with a grip on the
slippery seabed.

Tusks are
upside-down
on this skeleton

THE FOSSIL RECORD *right*
Fossil skeletons, like this one of a giant
mammoth, are often the only evidence
we have of animals now long extinct.

Spiny scallop shell

Mammals

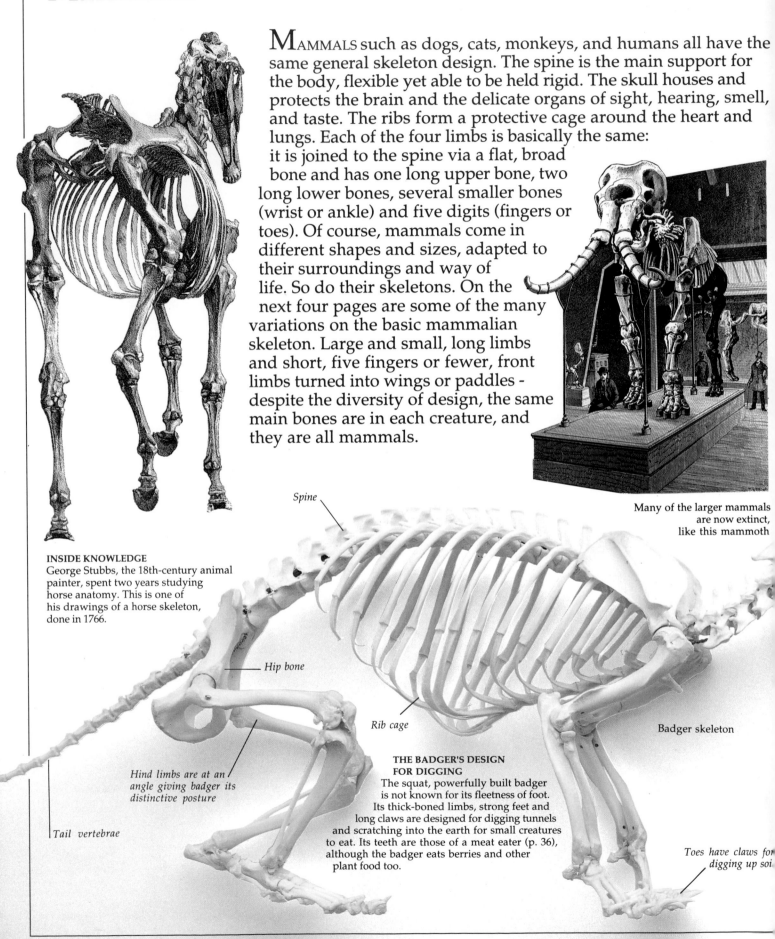

MAMMALS such as dogs, cats, monkeys, and humans all have the same general skeleton design. The spine is the main support for the body, flexible yet able to be held rigid. The skull houses and protects the brain and the delicate organs of sight, hearing, smell, and taste. The ribs form a protective cage around the heart and lungs. Each of the four limbs is basically the same: it is joined to the spine via a flat, broad bone and has one long upper bone, two long lower bones, several smaller bones (wrist or ankle) and five digits (fingers or toes). Of course, mammals come in different shapes and sizes, adapted to their surroundings and way of life. So do their skeletons. On the next four pages are some of the many variations on the basic mammalian skeleton. Large and small, long limbs and short, five fingers or fewer, front limbs turned into wings or paddles - despite the diversity of design, the same main bones are in each creature, and they are all mammals.

Many of the larger mammals are now extinct, like this mammoth

INSIDE KNOWLEDGE
George Stubbs, the 18th-century animal painter, spent two years studying horse anatomy. This is one of his drawings of a horse skeleton, done in 1766.

Spine

Hip bone

Rib cage

Badger skeleton

Hind limbs are at an angle giving badger its distinctive posture

Tail vertebrae

THE BADGER'S DESIGN FOR DIGGING
The squat, powerfully built badger is not known for its fleetness of foot. Its thick-boned limbs, strong feet and long claws are designed for digging tunnels and scratching into the earth for small creatures to eat. Its teeth are those of a meat eater (p. 36), although the badger eats berries and other plant food too.

Toes have claws for digging up soil

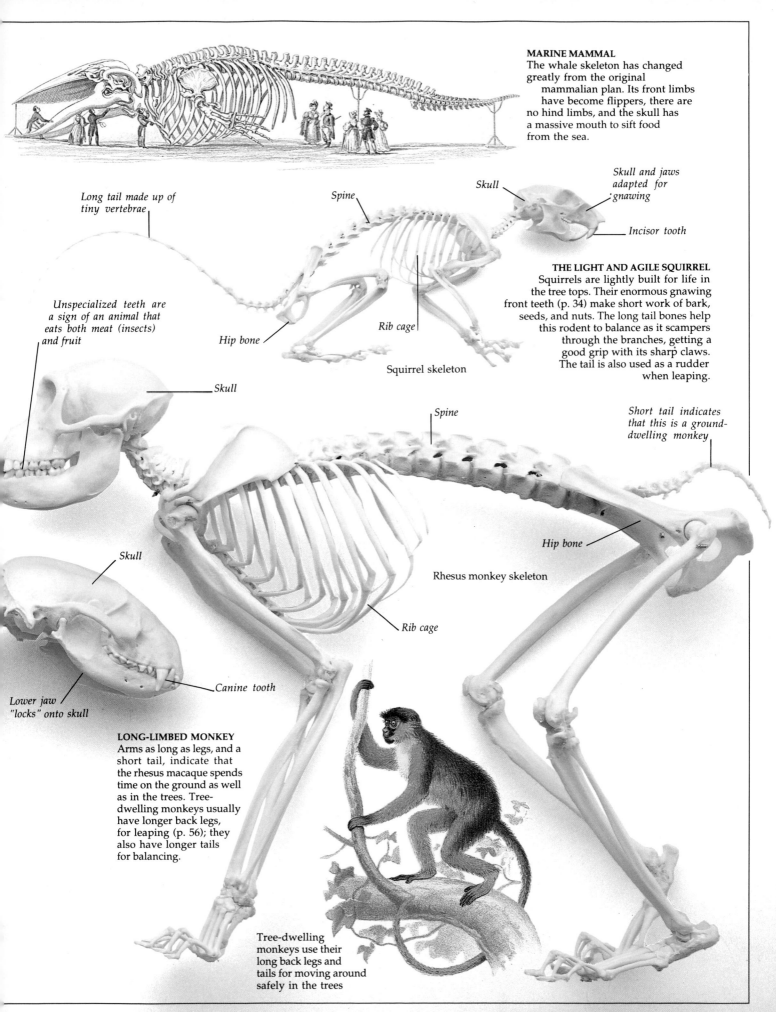

MARINE MAMMAL
The whale skeleton has changed greatly from the original mammalian plan. Its front limbs have become flippers, there are no hind limbs, and the skull has a massive mouth to sift food from the sea.

Long tail made up of tiny vertebrae

Spine

Skull

Skull and jaws adapted for gnawing

Incisor tooth

Unspecialized teeth are a sign of an animal that eats both meat (insects) and fruit

Hip bone

Rib cage

Squirrel skeleton

THE LIGHT AND AGILE SQUIRREL
Squirrels are lightly built for life in the tree tops. Their enormous gnawing front teeth (p. 34) make short work of bark, seeds, and nuts. The long tail bones help this rodent to balance as it scampers through the branches, getting a good grip with its sharp claws. The tail is also used as a rudder when leaping.

Skull

Spine

Short tail indicates that this is a ground-dwelling monkey

Skull

Hip bone

Rhesus monkey skeleton

Rib cage

Lower jaw "locks" onto skull

Canine tooth

LONG-LIMBED MONKEY
Arms as long as legs, and a short tail, indicate that the rhesus macaque spends time on the ground as well as in the trees. Tree-dwelling monkeys usually have longer back legs, for leaping (p. 56); they also have longer tails for balancing.

Tree-dwelling monkeys use their long back legs and tails for moving around safely in the trees

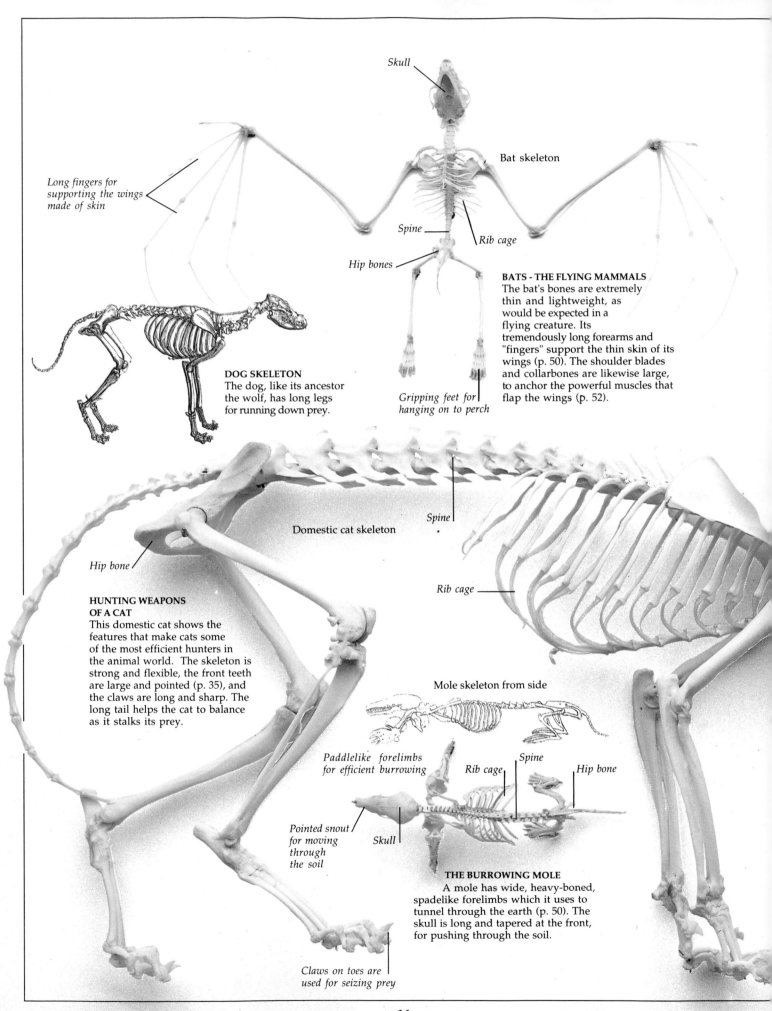

Skull

Bat skeleton

Long fingers for
supporting the wings
made of skin

Spine

Rib cage

Hip bones

BATS - THE FLYING MAMMALS
The bat's bones are extremely
thin and lightweight, as
would be expected in a
flying creature. Its
tremendously long forearms and
"fingers" support the thin skin of its
wings (p. 50). The shoulder blades
and collarbones are likewise large,
to anchor the powerful muscles that
flap the wings (p. 52).

Gripping feet for
hanging on to perch

DOG SKELETON
The dog, like its ancestor
the wolf, has long legs
for running down prey.

Spine

Domestic cat skeleton

Hip bone

Rib cage

**HUNTING WEAPONS
OF A CAT**
This domestic cat shows the
features that make cats some
of the most efficient hunters in
the animal world. The skeleton is
strong and flexible, the front teeth
are large and pointed (p. 35), and
the claws are long and sharp. The
long tail helps the cat to balance
as it stalks its prey.

Mole skeleton from side

Paddlelike forelimbs
for efficient burrowing

Rib cage

Spine

Hip bone

Pointed snout
for moving
through
the soil

Skull

THE BURROWING MOLE
A mole has wide, heavy-boned,
spadelike forelimbs which it uses to
tunnel through the earth (p. 50). The
skull is long and tapered at the front,
for pushing through the soil.

Claws on toes are
used for seizing prey

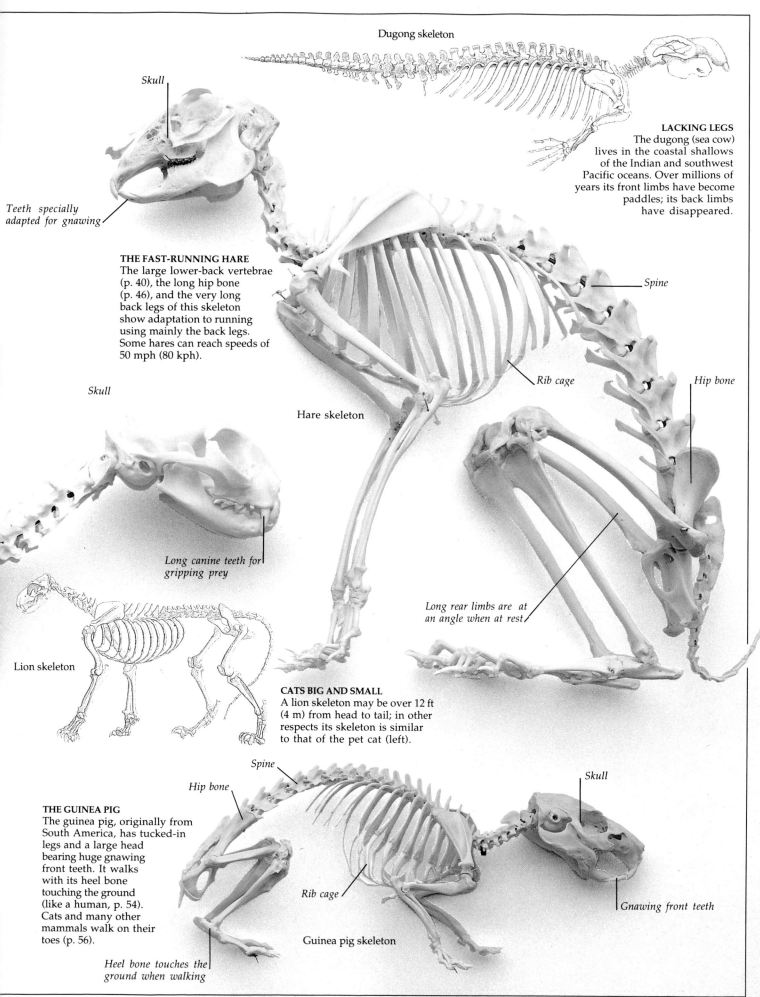

Dugong skeleton

Skull

*Teeth specially
adapted for gnawing*

LACKING LEGS
The dugong (sea cow)
lives in the coastal shallows
of the Indian and southwest
Pacific oceans. Over millions of
years its front limbs have become
paddles; its back limbs
have disappeared.

THE FAST-RUNNING HARE
The large lower-back vertebrae
(p. 40), the long hip bone
(p. 46), and the very long
back legs of this skeleton
show adaptation to running
using mainly the back legs.
Some hares can reach speeds of
50 mph (80 kph).

Spine

Skull

Rib cage

Hip bone

Hare skeleton

*Long canine teeth for
gripping prey*

*Long rear limbs are at
an angle when at rest*

Lion skeleton

CATS BIG AND SMALL
A lion skeleton may be over 12 ft
(4 m) from head to tail; in other
respects its skeleton is similar
to that of the pet cat (left).

Spine

Skull

Hip bone

THE GUINEA PIG
The guinea pig, originally from
South America, has tucked-in
legs and a large head
bearing huge gnawing
front teeth. It walks
with its heel bone
touching the ground
(like a human, p. 54).
Cats and many other
mammals walk on their
toes (p. 56).

Rib cage

Gnawing front teeth

Guinea pig skeleton

*Heel bone touches the
ground when walking*

Birds

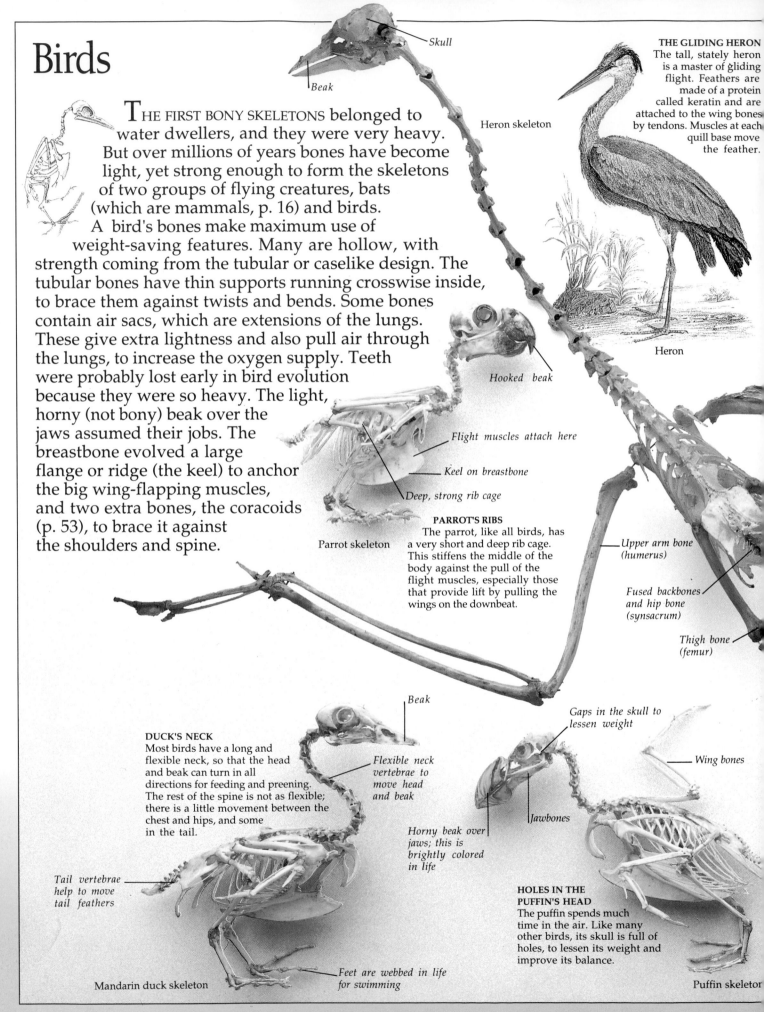

THE FIRST BONY SKELETONS belonged to water dwellers, and they were very heavy. But over millions of years bones have become light, yet strong enough to form the skeletons of two groups of flying creatures, bats (which are mammals, p. 16) and birds.

A bird's bones make maximum use of weight-saving features. Many are hollow, with strength coming from the tubular or caselike design. The tubular bones have thin supports running crosswise inside, to brace them against twists and bends. Some bones contain air sacs, which are extensions of the lungs. These give extra lightness and also pull air through the lungs, to increase the oxygen supply. Teeth were probably lost early in bird evolution because they were so heavy. The light, horny (not bony) beak over the jaws assumed their jobs. The breastbone evolved a large flange or ridge (the keel) to anchor the big wing-flapping muscles, and two extra bones, the coracoids (p. 53), to brace it against the shoulders and spine.

Skull

Beak

Heron skeleton

THE GLIDING HERON
The tall, stately heron is a master of gliding flight. Feathers are made of a protein called keratin and are attached to the wing bones by tendons. Muscles at each quill base move the feather.

Heron

Hooked beak

Flight muscles attach here

Keel on breastbone

Deep, strong rib cage

PARROT'S RIBS
The parrot, like all birds, has a very short and deep rib cage. This stiffens the middle of the body against the pull of the flight muscles, especially those that provide lift by pulling the wings on the downbeat.

Parrot skeleton

Upper arm bone (humerus)

Fused backbones and hip bone (synsacrum)

Thigh bone (femur)

Beak

DUCK'S NECK
Most birds have a long and flexible neck, so that the head and beak can turn in all directions for feeding and preening. The rest of the spine is not as flexible; there is a little movement between the chest and hips, and some in the tail.

Flexible neck vertebrae to move head and beak

Tail vertebrae help to move tail feathers

Feet are webbed in life for swimming

Mandarin duck skeleton

Gaps in the skull to lessen weight

Wing bones

Jawbones

Horny beak over jaws; this is brightly colored in life

HOLES IN THE PUFFIN'S HEAD
The puffin spends much time in the air. Like many other birds, its skull is full of holes, to lessen its weight and improve its balance.

Puffin skeleton

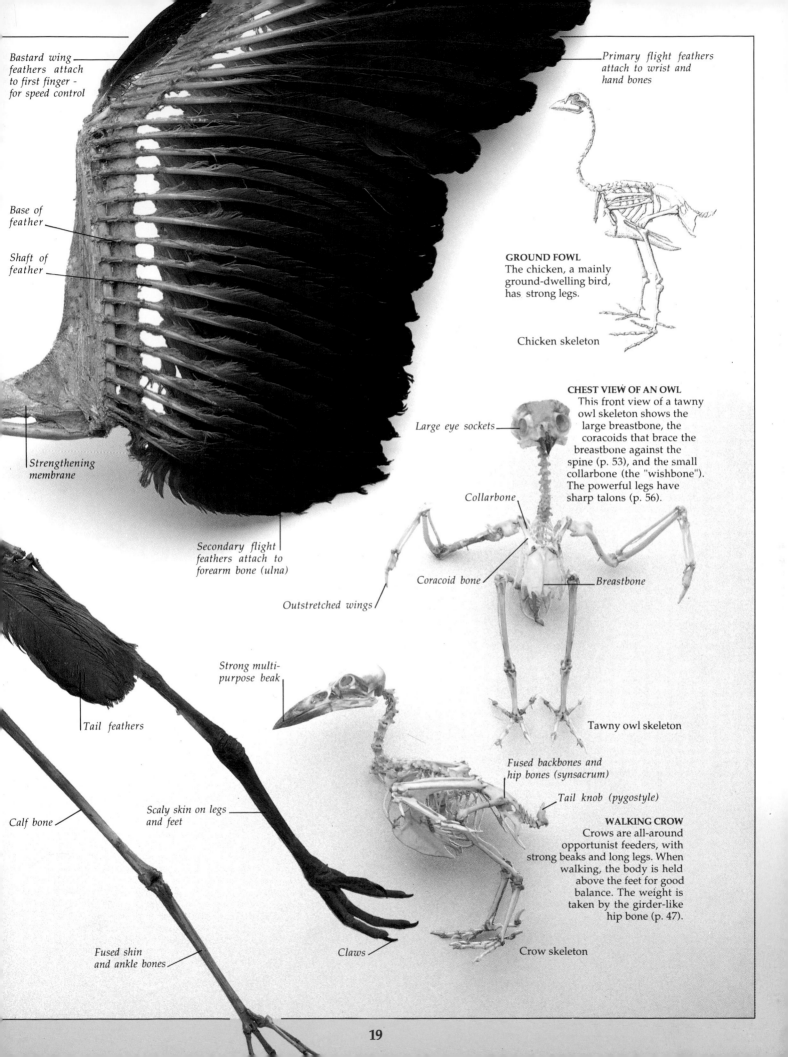

Bastard wing feathers attach to first finger - for speed control

Base of feather

Shaft of feather

Strengthening membrane

Secondary flight feathers attach to forearm bone (ulna)

Primary flight feathers attach to wrist and hand bones

GROUND FOWL
The chicken, a mainly ground-dwelling bird, has strong legs.

Chicken skeleton

CHEST VIEW OF AN OWL
This front view of a tawny owl skeleton shows the large breastbone, the coracoids that brace the breastbone against the spine (p. 53), and the small collarbone (the "wishbone"). The powerful legs have sharp talons (p. 56).

Large eye sockets

Collarbone

Coracoid bone

Breastbone

Outstretched wings

Tawny owl skeleton

Tail feathers

Strong multi-purpose beak

Scaly skin on legs and feet

Calf bone

Fused shin and ankle bones

Claws

Fused backbones and hip bones (synsacrum)

Tail knob (pygostyle)

WALKING CROW
Crows are all-around opportunist feeders, with strong beaks and long legs. When walking, the body is held above the feet for good balance. The weight is taken by the girder-like hip bone (p. 47).

Crow skeleton

Fish, reptiles, and amphibians

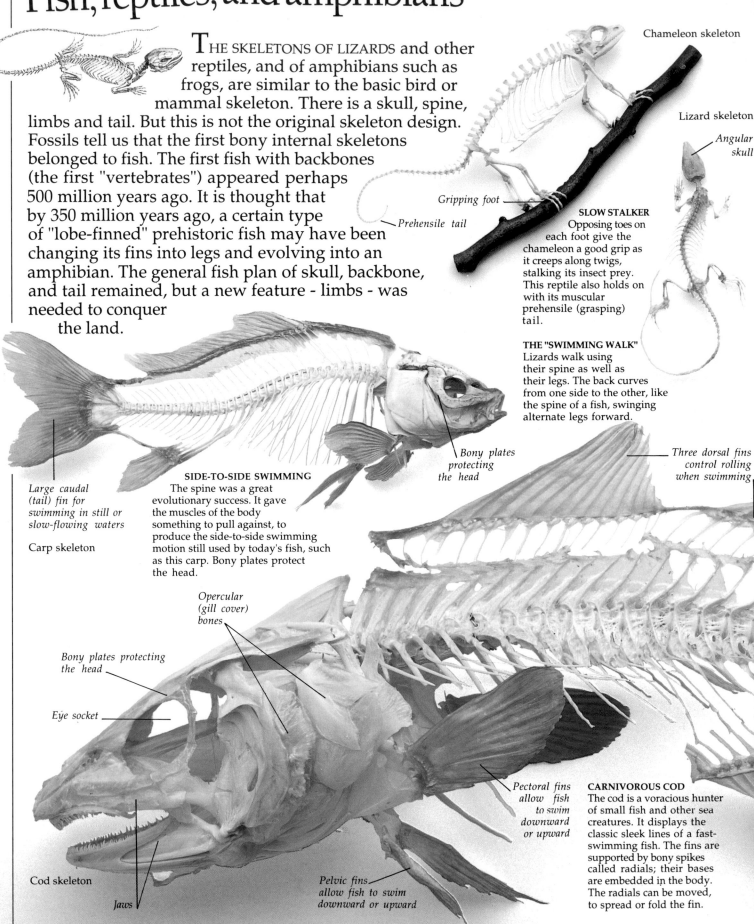

THE SKELETONS OF LIZARDS and other reptiles, and of amphibians such as frogs, are similar to the basic bird or mammal skeleton. There is a skull, spine, limbs and tail. But this is not the original skeleton design. Fossils tell us that the first bony internal skeletons belonged to fish. The first fish with backbones (the first "vertebrates") appeared perhaps 500 million years ago. It is thought that by 350 million years ago, a certain type of "lobe-finned" prehistoric fish may have been changing its fins into legs and evolving into an amphibian. The general fish plan of skull, backbone, and tail remained, but a new feature - limbs - was needed to conquer the land.

Chameleon skeleton

Lizard skeleton

Angular skull

Gripping foot

Prehensile tail

SLOW STALKER
Opposing toes on each foot give the chameleon a good grip as it creeps along twigs, stalking its insect prey. This reptile also holds on with its muscular prehensile (grasping) tail.

THE "SWIMMING WALK"
Lizards walk using their spine as well as their legs. The back curves from one side to the other, like the spine of a fish, swinging alternate legs forward.

Bony plates protecting the head

Three dorsal fins control rolling when swimming

SIDE-TO-SIDE SWIMMING
The spine was a great evolutionary success. It gave the muscles of the body something to pull against, to produce the side-to-side swimming motion still used by today's fish, such as this carp. Bony plates protect the head.

Large caudal (tail) fin for swimming in still or slow-flowing waters

Carp skeleton

Opercular (gill cover) bones

Bony plates protecting the head

Eye socket

Pectoral fins allow fish to swim downward or upward

CARNIVOROUS COD
The cod is a voracious hunter of small fish and other sea creatures. It displays the classic sleek lines of a fast-swimming fish. The fins are supported by bony spikes called radials; their bases are embedded in the body. The radials can be moved, to spread or fold the fin.

Cod skeleton

Jaws

Pelvic fins allow fish to swim downward or upward

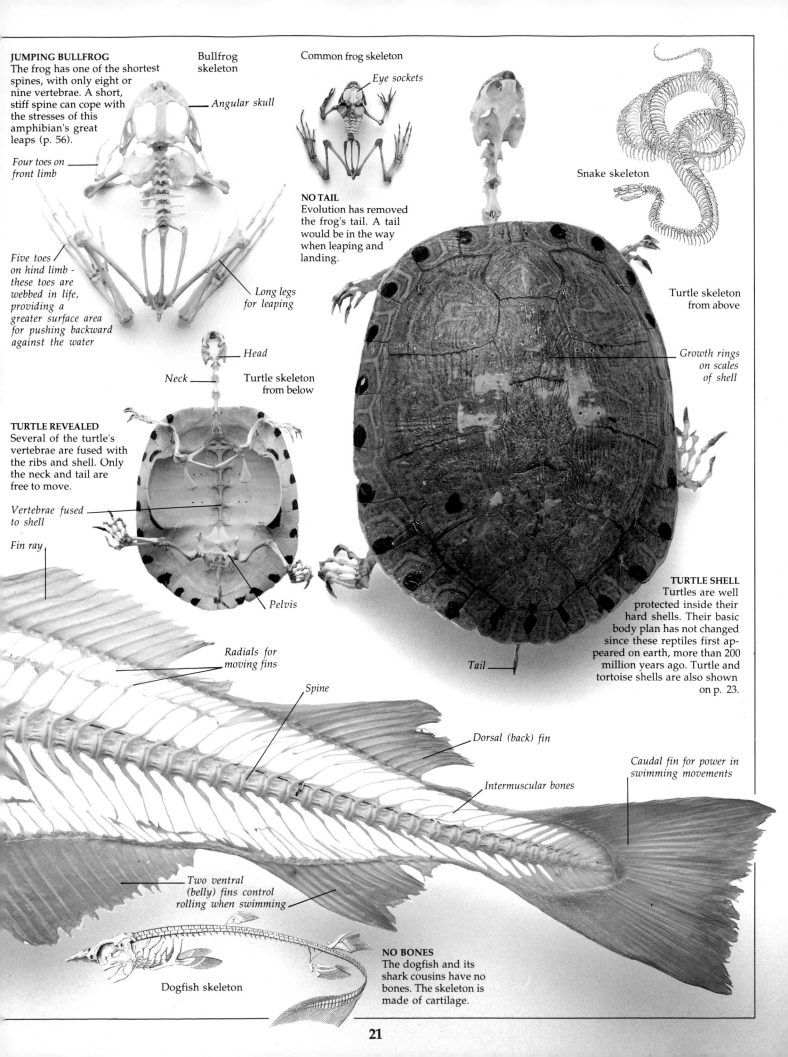

JUMPING BULLFROG
The frog has one of the shortest spines, with only eight or nine vertebrae. A short, stiff spine can cope with the stresses of this amphibian's great leaps (p. 56).

Four toes on front limb

Five toes on hind limb - these toes are webbed in life, providing a greater surface area for pushing backward against the water

Bullfrog skeleton

Angular skull

Common frog skeleton

Eye sockets

NO TAIL
Evolution has removed the frog's tail. A tail would be in the way when leaping and landing.

Long legs for leaping

Snake skeleton

Turtle skeleton from above

Head

Neck

Turtle skeleton from below

Growth rings on scales of shell

TURTLE REVEALED
Several of the turtle's vertebrae are fused with the ribs and shell. Only the neck and tail are free to move.

Vertebrae fused to shell

Fin ray

Radials for moving fins

Pelvis

Spine

TURTLE SHELL
Turtles are well protected inside their hard shells. Their basic body plan has not changed since these reptiles first appeared on earth, more than 200 million years ago. Turtle and tortoise shells are also shown on p. 23.

Tail

Dorsal (back) fin

Intermuscular bones

Caudal fin for power in swimming movements

Two ventral (belly) fins control rolling when swimming

Dogfish skeleton

NO BONES
The dogfish and its shark cousins have no bones. The skeleton is made of cartilage.

21

Skeletons on the outside

THE VAST MAJORITY of animals do not have a bony internal skeleton. Insects, spiders, shellfish, and other invertebrates (animals with no backbone) have a hard outer casing called an exoskeleton. This exoskeleton does the same job as an internal skeleton, providing strength and support. It also forms a hard, protective shield around the soft inner organs. But it does have drawbacks. It cannot expand, so the animal must grow by molting (shedding) its old exoskeleton and making a new, larger one. Above a certain size it becomes so thick and heavy that the muscles cannot move it. This is why animals with exoskeletons tend to be small.

Magnification X40

MICROSKELETONS
Diatoms float by the billions in the oceans. Like plants, these single-celled algae trap the sun's light energy to grow. They construct silica casings around themselves, presumably for protection. These "skeletons" are amazingly elaborate and beautiful in shape and variety.

WOOD-BORING BEETLE
This metallic purple and yellow beetle has a larva that bores under the bark of trees.

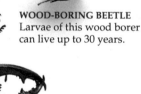

WOOD-BORING BEETLE
Larvae of this wood borer can live up to 30 years.

WOOD-BORING BEETLE
The larva of this brilliant green beetle can be a serious timber pest.

LEAF BEETLE
A brilliant green exoskeleton camouflages these beetles among leaves.

DUNG BEETLE
This beetle makes a dung-filled burrow as food for its young.

STAG BEETLE
The male cannot bite hard - his jaw muscles are too weak.

DARKLING BEETLE
Long antennae help this beetle feel its way around.

ALLOVER ARMOR
Like other insects, beetles are well protected by a tough exoskeleton made of a hard, waterproof material called chitin. The wing cases were once another pair of wings, since modified by evolution. This goliath beetle is the heaviest insect, weighing 3.5 oz (100 g).

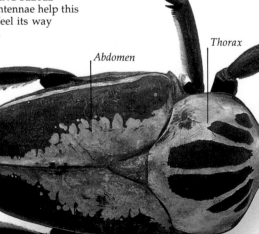

Abdomen

Thorax

Head

Eye

Jointed limb

Wing case

Goliath beetle

Leg muscles are inside tubular leg skeleton

Transparent wing

THE WINGS REVEALED
Under the hard outer wing cases lie the delicate, transparent wings used for flight. The long legs have many joints.

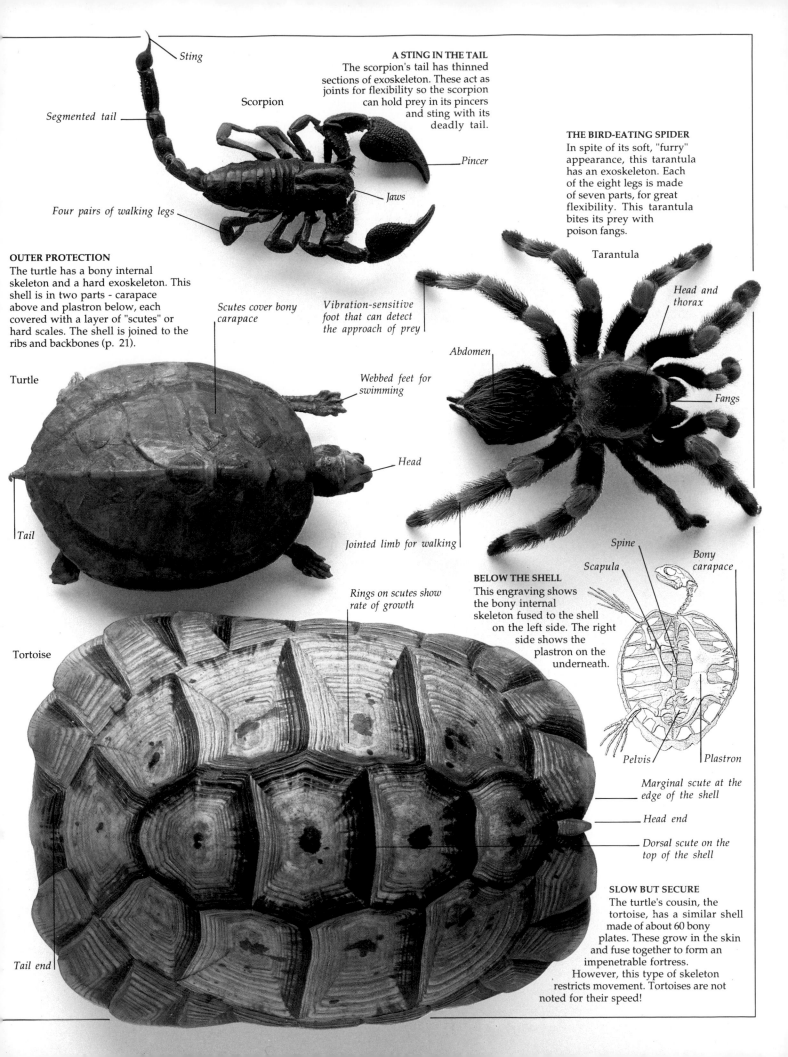

Sting

Segmented tail

Scorpion

A STING IN THE TAIL
The scorpion's tail has thinned sections of exoskeleton. These act as joints for flexibility so the scorpion can hold prey in its pincers and sting with its deadly tail.

Pincer

Jaws

Four pairs of walking legs

THE BIRD-EATING SPIDER
In spite of its soft, "furry" appearance, this tarantula has an exoskeleton. Each of the eight legs is made of seven parts, for great flexibility. This tarantula bites its prey with poison fangs.

Tarantula

Head and thorax

OUTER PROTECTION
The turtle has a bony internal skeleton and a hard exoskeleton. This shell is in two parts - carapace above and plastron below, each covered with a layer of "scutes" or hard scales. The shell is joined to the ribs and backbones (p. 21).

Scutes cover bony carapace

Vibration-sensitive foot that can detect the approach of prey

Abdomen

Fangs

Turtle

Webbed feet for swimming

Head

Tail

Jointed limb for walking

Spine

Scapula

Bony carapace

BELOW THE SHELL
This engraving shows the bony internal skeleton fused to the shell on the left side. The right side shows the plastron on the underneath.

Rings on scutes show rate of growth

Tortoise

Pelvis

Plastron

Marginal scute at the edge of the shell

Head end

Dorsal scute on the top of the shell

SLOW BUT SECURE
The turtle's cousin, the tortoise, has a similar shell made of about 60 bony plates. These grow in the skin and fuse together to form an impenetrable fortress. However, this type of skeleton restricts movement. Tortoises are not noted for their speed!

Tail end

Marine exoskeletons

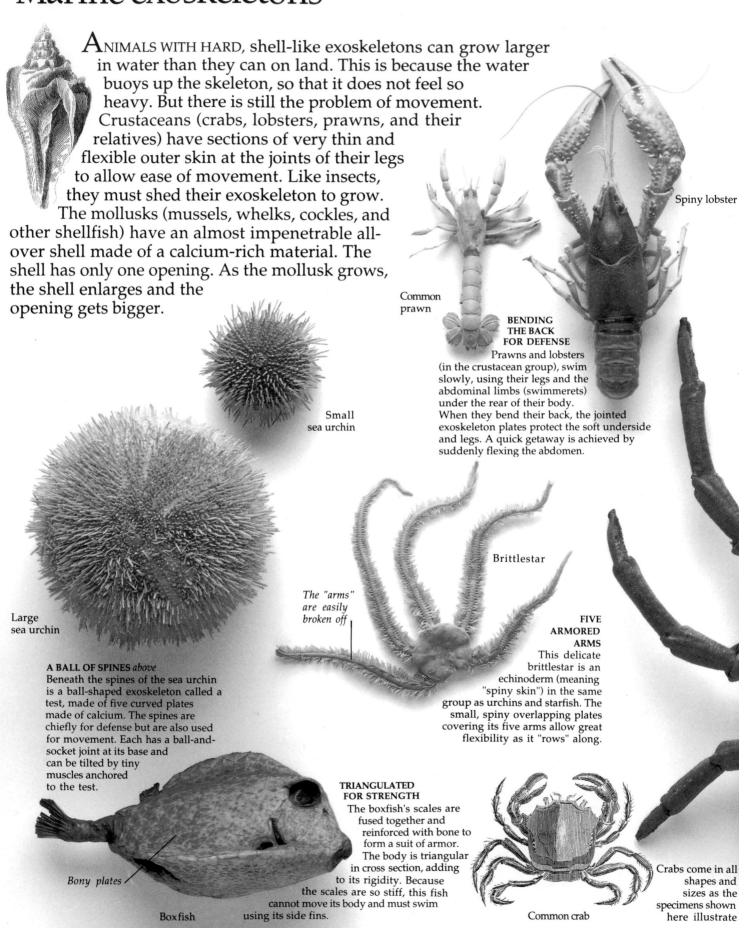

ANIMALS WITH HARD, shell-like exoskeletons can grow larger in water than they can on land. This is because the water buoys up the skeleton, so that it does not feel so heavy. But there is still the problem of movement. Crustaceans (crabs, lobsters, prawns, and their relatives) have sections of very thin and flexible outer skin at the joints of their legs to allow ease of movement. Like insects, they must shed their exoskeleton to grow. The mollusks (mussels, whelks, cockles, and other shellfish) have an almost impenetrable all-over shell made of a calcium-rich material. The shell has only one opening. As the mollusk grows, the shell enlarges and the opening gets bigger.

Spiny lobster

Common prawn

BENDING THE BACK FOR DEFENSE
Prawns and lobsters (in the crustacean group), swim slowly, using their legs and the abdominal limbs (swimmerets) under the rear of their body. When they bend their back, the jointed exoskeleton plates protect the soft underside and legs. A quick getaway is achieved by suddenly flexing the abdomen.

Small sea urchin

Large sea urchin

Brittlestar

The "arms" are easily broken off

FIVE ARMORED ARMS
This delicate brittlestar is an echinoderm (meaning "spiny skin") in the same group as urchins and starfish. The small, spiny overlapping plates covering its five arms allow great flexibility as it "rows" along.

A BALL OF SPINES *above*
Beneath the spines of the sea urchin is a ball-shaped exoskeleton called a test, made of five curved plates made of calcium. The spines are chiefly for defense but are also used for movement. Each has a ball-and-socket joint at its base and can be tilted by tiny muscles anchored to the test.

TRIANGULATED FOR STRENGTH
The boxfish's scales are fused together and reinforced with bone to form a suit of armor. The body is triangular in cross section, adding to its rigidity. Because the scales are so stiff, this fish cannot move its body and must swim using its side fins.

Bony plates

Boxfish

Common crab

Crabs come in all shapes and sizes as the specimens shown here illustrate

Seen upside down, the starfish reveals its central mouth

Precious wentletrap

Nautilus

Starfish

Money cowries

ARMS WITH FEET
Beneath the starfish's arms are small holes. Tiny "tube feet" poke through them. They wave to and fro and have suckers at the ends. The starfish walks using these tube feet; its plated arms are much less flexible.

Masked crab

The ridges on the shell look like a face mask

SEASHORE SHELLS
Mollusks such as the nautilus and the wentletrap have a coiled shell for an outer skeleton. To grow, the animal adds another coil, or whorl. The adult cowrie's whorl wraps around the whole shell.

Entrance to shell

Prickly cockle

A COCKLE'S MUSCLES
The sand-dwelling cockle has a pair of thick, ribbed shells to protect it from the pounding surf and shore rocks. The two shells, or valves, are opened and closed by strong muscles.

Claw

Eye

The exoskeleton has many joints

Spiny spider crab

Seahorse

Prehensile tail

CHANGING SKELETONS
A crab must crawl out of its old exoskeleton when this becomes too small - right down to its last leg and antenna. Quickly the crab's soft body expands, then a fresh exoskeleton hardens over it. The molt takes several hours, during which the vulnerable creature hides in a crack or under a boulder.

Hermit crab

USING CASTOFFS
The hermit crab protects its soft body in a castoff mollusk shell.

BONY OUTER COVERING
The strange-looking seahorse is a true fish, but it swims upright. An armor of bony rings encases its body, and its fins provide movement. The prehensile tail grasps seaweed when at rest.

The human skull and teeth

ALTHOUGH THE HEAD is at one end of the human body, it functions as the body's center. The skull protects the brain, which is the central coordinator for receiving information from the outside world and organizing the body's reactions. The special senses of sight, hearing, smell, and taste are concentrated in the skull. In particular, the eyes and inner ears (where the delicate organs of hearing are sited) lie well protected in bony recesses. Air, containing the oxygen vital to life, passes through the skull by way of the nose and mouth. Food is crushed first by the jaws and teeth so that it can be swallowed and digested more easily. The senses of smell and taste are well positioned to check air and food for harmful odors and flavors.

THIS WON'T HURT ...
Teeth are both tough and sensitive. A visit to a medieval dentist was a painful affair, but it would hopefully give merciful relief from long-term nagging toothache.

A COLORED SKULL
A computer-colored x-ray shows the bones in the skull and neck. The soft tissues of the nose, which is not made of bone, also show up.

Incisor tooth

Canine tooth

Premolar tooth

Roof of mouth

Molar tooth

Nasal passages and sinuses

Lower jaw fits here

Outer ear canal

Hole for carotid artery

Uppermost vertebra fits here

Hole for spinal cord

THE BASE OF THE SKULL
This unfamiliar underview of the skull, with the lower jaw removed, shows the delicate internal sectioning. (The individual bones of the skull are identified on pages 28-29.)

BRAINCASE
The delicate brain tissue is surrounded by a bony case. Its internal volume is some 2.5 pints (about 1,500 cc).

EYE HOLE
The eye socket, or orbit, protects the eyeball, which is a sphere about 1 in (25 mm) across. The socket is larger; sandwiched between the eyeball and the socket are cushioning pads of fat, nerves, and blood vessels, and the muscles that move the eye.

NERVE HOLE
Many nerves lead to and from the brain through holes in the skull. This hole, the infra-orbital foramen, is for nerve branches from the upper incisor, canine and premolar teeth.

NOSE HOLE
The protruding hump of the human nose is made of cartilage, not bone, so it is absent from the skeleton of the skull.

TOOTH HOLES
The bone of the jaw is spongy in texture and anchors the roots of the teeth.

The teeth

An adult human has 32 teeth. In each jaw (upper and lower) there are four incisors at the front then, on each side, one canine, two premolars, and three molars. The enamel of a tooth is the hardest substance in the body.

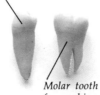
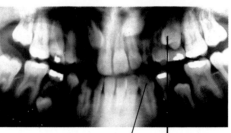

Incisor tooth for cutting and snipping

Premolar tooth for crushing and chewing

Canine tooth for piercing and tearing

Molar tooth for crushing and chewing

INSIDE A TOOTH *right*
If a tooth is sliced open, various layers can be clearly seen inside. The outer layer is enamel, a hard, protective substance. Under this is a tough layer of dentine, which surrounds the pulp. Pulp contains nerves and blood vessels.

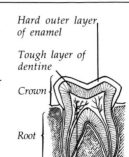

Hard outer layer of enamel

Tough layer of dentine

Crown

Root

Nerves and blood vessels of pulp

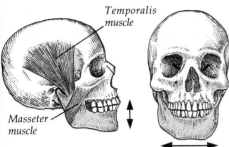

Temporalis muscle

Masseter muscle

ALL-AROUND CHEWING *above*
As we eat, the lower jaw moves up and down, and also from side to side, and even from front to back, for a really thorough chewing job. The tongue (which is almost all muscle) moves the food around the mouth; the cheek muscles keep food pressed between the teeth.

GROWING TEETH *right*
A young child has a set of 20 milk (deciduous) teeth. (Small jaws cannot hold more than that.) They fall out from the age of about six years, starting with those at the front.

"Wraparound" x-ray of child's teeth

Milk tooth

Permanent tooth developing in gum

BRAIN DOME
The human forehead is more dome-shaped and bulging than that of our ape relatives. It houses the cerebral cortex - the part of the brain associated with intelligence.

SHUTTING THE MOUTH
The broad, flat side of the skull acts as the attachment point for the upper end of the powerful temporalis muscle, an important chewing muscle (above).

BITING AND CHEWING
The lower end of the temporalis muscle joins to this part of the lower jawbone.

EAR HOLE
The ear canal leads inward from the outer ear, which is made of cartilage. The organs of hearing in the inner ear are embedded deep within the skull bone.

JAW JOINT
This joint is quite mobile - you can open and close your mouth, stick out your chin and move it from side to side.

CHEEKBONE
The cheekbone is made from two bones, the zygomatic and a finger-like projection from the temporal (p. 29). It protects the lower eyeball and anchors the upper end of the masseter muscle, one of the main chewing muscles (above).

GLASS JAW
A sudden knock to the chin is transmitted up through the rigid jaw-bone in to the skull, shaking the brain violently inside its cushioning membranes (the meninges). This can result in unconsciousness - a knockout.

27

How the skull is built

THE HUMAN SKULL STARTS LIFE as an intricate curved jigsaw of nearly 30 separate pieces, sculpted in cartilage and membrane. During development these gradually turn to bone and grow together to form a solid case that protects the brain, eyes, inner ears, and other delicate sense organs. The separate bones are eventually knitted together with fibrous tissue. These joins, or "sutures", can be seen as wiggly lines on the skull. From the age of about 30 to 40 years, the sutures slowly fade and disappear. This is one way of telling the age of a skull's original owner. The cranium, or "brainbox," is made up of eight bones. There are 14 in the face, two on each side of the upper jaw, and one in each side of the lower jaw. The skull also encases the smallest bones in the body—the six tiny ossicles of the inner ears—three on each side of the skull (p.59).

A SKELETON PONDERS A SKULL
This engraving by the Belgian Vesalius (1514-64), the founding father of anatomy, is thought to have been Shakespeare's inspiration for the graveyard scene in *Hamlet*.

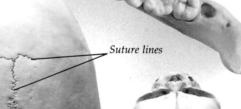

Two maxillae bear the top teeth and form the roof of the mouth

Inferior concha warms and moistens air as it enters the nose

The palatine bone makes up the back of the roof of the mouth

The lower back of the nasal cavity is called the vomer

The mandible, or lower jaw, consists of two firmly joined halves

The nasal bones make up the bridge of the nose

Inferior concha

Palatine bone

Maxilla

The fontaneles

During birth, the baby's head is squeezed as it passes along the birth canal (p. 45). Fontaneles are "soft spots" in the baby's skull, where the membrane has not yet turned to bone. They allow the skull bones to mold, slide, and even overlap, to minimize damage to the skull and brain. The largest of the six fontaneles is on the top of the skull. They disappear by one year of age.

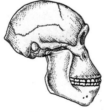

Suture lines

Adult skull

Baby's skull

The pulsing of the baby's blood system can often be seen beneath the thin membrane layer of the uppermost fontanele.

The flattening face

Fossils found so far give us a broad outline of how the human skull may have evolved. Some of our probable ancestors are shown on the right. Gradually the face has become flatter, the teeth smaller, the chin less protruding, and the forehead more domed, to house the increasingly large brain.

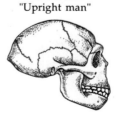

Australopithecus "Southern ape"

3-2 million years ago

Homo erectus "Upright man"

750,000 years ago

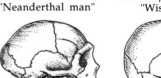

Homo sapiens neanderthalensis "Neanderthal man"

100,000-40,000 years ago

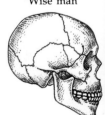

Homo sapiens sapiens "Wise man"

40,000 years ago to today

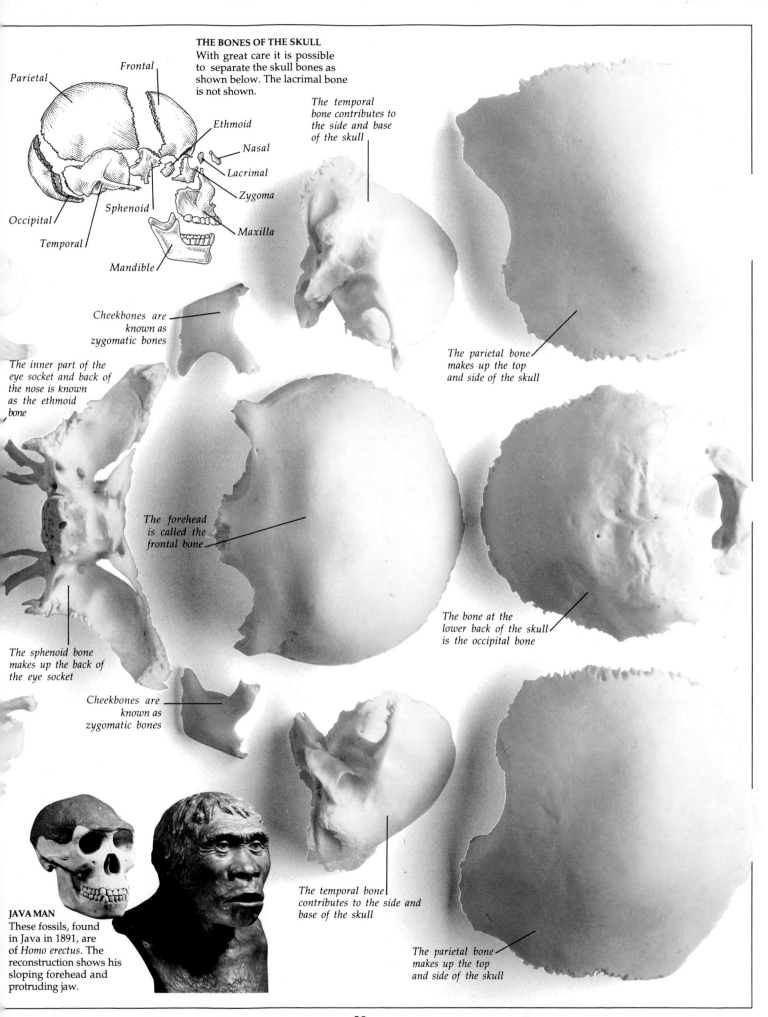

THE BONES OF THE SKULL
With great care it is possible to separate the skull bones as shown below. The lacrimal bone is not shown.

Parietal

Frontal

Ethmoid

Nasal

Lacrimal

Zygoma

Maxilla

Occipital

Sphenoid

Temporal

Mandible

The temporal bone contributes to the side and base of the skull

Cheekbones are known as zygomatic bones

The parietal bone makes up the top and side of the skull

The inner part of the eye socket and back of the nose is known as the ethmoid bone

The forehead is called the frontal bone

The bone at the lower back of the skull is the occipital bone

The sphenoid bone makes up the back of the eye socket

Cheekbones are known as zygomatic bones

The temporal bone contributes to the side and base of the skull

The parietal bone makes up the top and side of the skull

JAVA MAN
These fossils, found in Java in 1891, are of *Homo erectus*. The reconstruction shows his sloping forehead and protruding jaw.

Animal skulls

Each species of animal has a characteristic skull shape, molded by evolution to suit its particular way of life. Some skulls are light, with weight-saving gaps; others are thick and strong. Some are long and pointed, for probing and poking into holes; others are short and broad. All the skulls shown here have jaws: this may not seem very remarkable, but, in fact, jaws were a great step forward when they first evolved, in fish about 450 million years ago. They enabled their owners to catch large chunks of food and break it into pieces small enough to swallow. Before this, fish were jawless and restricted to sucking or sifting food from the mud.

BIRDS AND BILLS
The typical bird skull is very light, with large eye sockets and a small, rounded case at the back for the brain.

GANNET
A powerful bird with a long, streamlined bill, the gannet dives from on high for fish.

AVOCET
Upturned bill for sifting sea water.

TAWNY OWL
Wide skull to house enormous eyes.

AMAZON PARROT
A massive hooked bill shows its seed-cracking power.

MERGANSER
This duck's notched bill grasps fish to eat.

BLACKBIRD
All-purpose bill for eating insects, worms, berries, and seeds.

CURLEW
Long bill probes for small creatures.

RABBIT
Its eyes are on the sides of its head, keeping an all-around watch for predators.

MALLARD
Wide, flattened bill "dabbles" in water for tiny bits of food.

HAMSTER
Gnaws at seeds and nuts with its large front teeth.

HEDGEHOG
Many, but similar, teeth indicate a diet of insects and other small animals.

FROG
Forward-facing eyes judge distance of prey for accurate hunting.

ARMADILLO
The long nose sniffs out ants and other small creatures.

THE LONG AND THE SHORT
In most kinds, or species, of animals, all individuals have a skull of much the same shape. All domestic dogs are one species, *Canis familiaris*. But over the centuries, people have selectively bred them for different features (below). Some have large, long skulls (usually working dogs) while smaller breeds tend to be more "decorative."

BADGER
Squat, heavy skull with long canine teeth point to a hunting way of life.

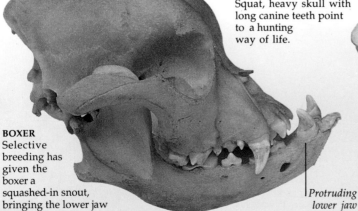

BOXER
Selective breeding has given the boxer a squashed-in snout, bringing the lower jaw to the front.

Protruding lower jaw

COLLIE
This breed has the more "natural" long muzzle of the dog's ancestor, the wolf.

Long muzzle

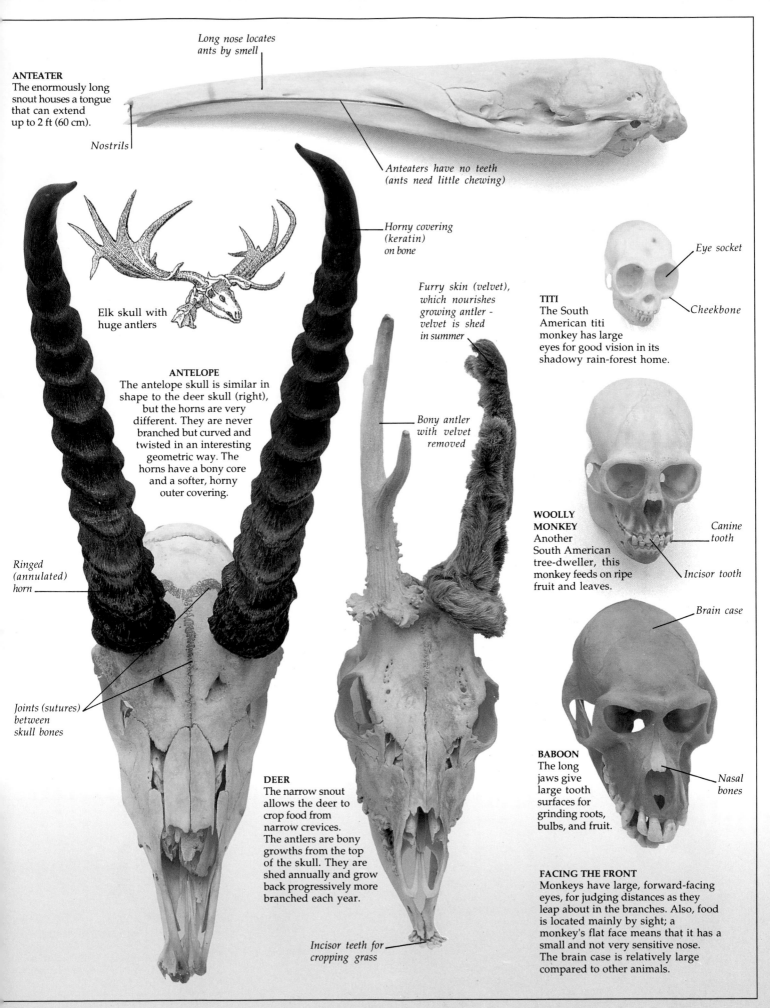

ANTEATER
The enormously long snout houses a tongue that can extend up to 2 ft (60 cm).

Long nose locates ants by smell

Nostrils

Anteaters have no teeth (ants need little chewing)

Horny covering (keratin) on bone

Elk skull with huge antlers

ANTELOPE
The antelope skull is similar in shape to the deer skull (right), but the horns are very different. They are never branched but curved and twisted in an interesting geometric way. The horns have a bony core and a softer, horny outer covering.

Furry skin (velvet), which nourishes growing antler - velvet is shed in summer

Bony antler with velvet removed

TITI
The South American titi monkey has large eyes for good vision in its shadowy rain-forest home.

Eye socket

Cheekbone

WOOLLY MONKEY
Another South American tree-dweller, this monkey feeds on ripe fruit and leaves.

Canine tooth

Incisor tooth

Ringed (annulated) horn

Joints (sutures) between skull bones

DEER
The narrow snout allows the deer to crop food from narrow crevices. The antlers are bony growths from the top of the skull. They are shed annually and grow back progressively more branched each year.

Incisor teeth for cropping grass

Brain case

BABOON
The long jaws give large tooth surfaces for grinding roots, bulbs, and fruit.

Nasal bones

FACING THE FRONT
Monkeys have large, forward-facing eyes, for judging distances as they leap about in the branches. Also, food is located mainly by sight; a monkey's flat face means that it has a small and not very sensitive nose. The brain case is relatively large compared to other animals.

Animal senses

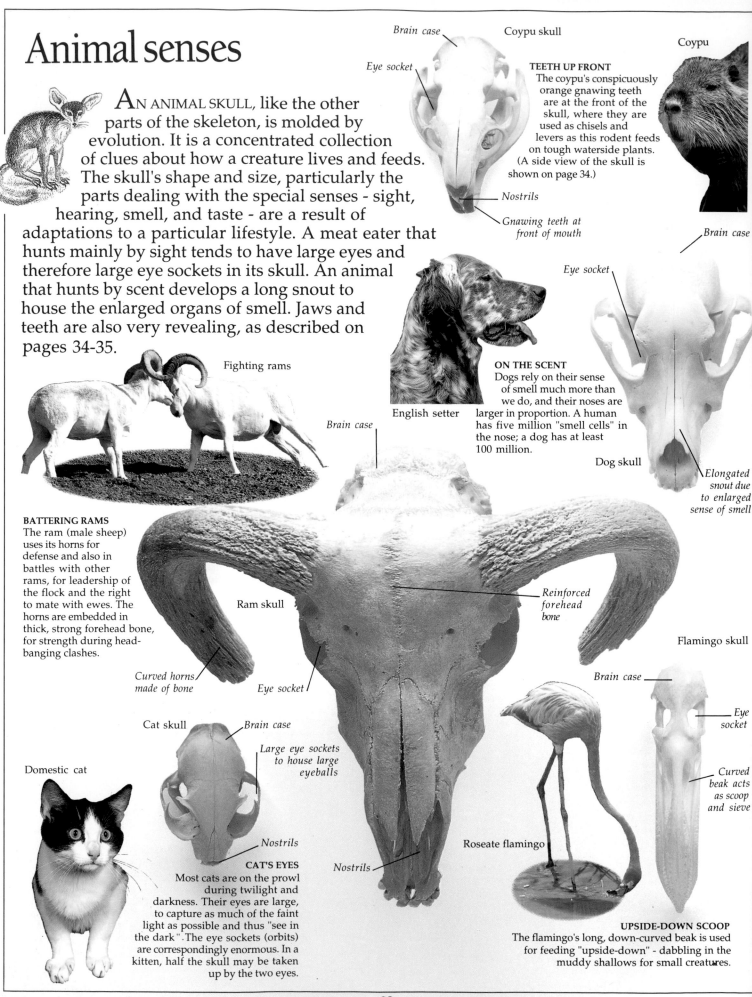

AN ANIMAL SKULL, like the other parts of the skeleton, is molded by evolution. It is a concentrated collection of clues about how a creature lives and feeds. The skull's shape and size, particularly the parts dealing with the special senses - sight, hearing, smell, and taste - are a result of adaptations to a particular lifestyle. A meat eater that hunts mainly by sight tends to have large eyes and therefore large eye sockets in its skull. An animal that hunts by scent develops a long snout to house the enlarged organs of smell. Jaws and teeth are also very revealing, as described on pages 34-35.

Coypu skull

Brain case

Eye socket

TEETH UP FRONT
The coypu's conspicuously orange gnawing teeth are at the front of the skull, where they are used as chisels and levers as this rodent feeds on tough waterside plants. (A side view of the skull is shown on page 34.)

Coypu

Nostrils

Gnawing teeth at front of mouth

Brain case

Eye socket

ON THE SCENT
Dogs rely on their sense of smell much more than we do, and their noses are larger in proportion. A human has five million "smell cells" in the nose; a dog has at least 100 million.

English setter

Dog skull

Elongated snout due to enlarged sense of smell

Fighting rams

BATTERING RAMS
The ram (male sheep) uses its horns for defense and also in battles with other rams, for leadership of the flock and the right to mate with ewes. The horns are embedded in thick, strong forehead bone, for strength during head-banging clashes.

Brain case

Ram skull

Reinforced forehead bone

Curved horns made of bone

Eye socket

Flamingo skull

Brain case

Eye socket

Curved beak acts as scoop and sieve

Cat skull

Brain case

Large eye sockets to house large eyeballs

Domestic cat

Nostrils

CAT'S EYES
Most cats are on the prowl during twilight and darkness. Their eyes are large, to capture as much of the faint light as possible and thus "see in the dark". The eye sockets (orbits) are correspondingly enormous. In a kitten, half the skull may be taken up by the two eyes.

Nostrils

Roseate flamingo

UPSIDE-DOWN SCOOP
The flamingo's long, down-curved beak is used for feeding "upside-down" - dabbling in the muddy shallows for small creatures.

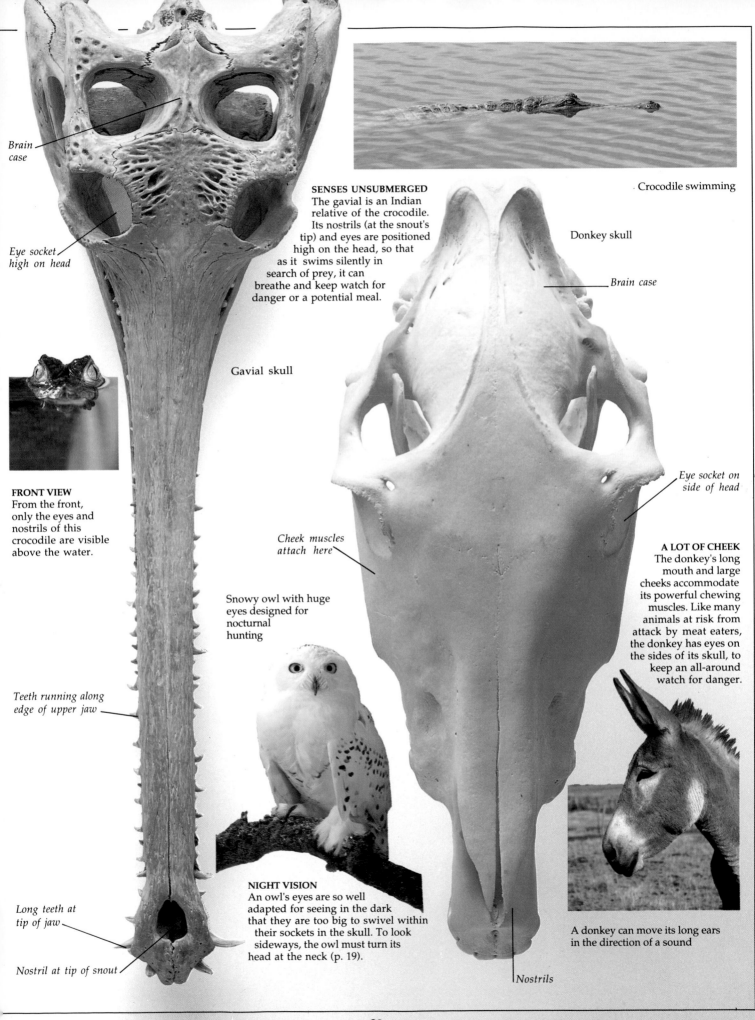

Brain
case

Eye socket
high on head

Crocodile swimming

SENSES UNSUBMERGED
The gavial is an Indian
relative of the crocodile.
Its nostrils (at the snout's
tip) and eyes are positioned
high on the head, so that
as it swims silently in
search of prey, it can
breathe and keep watch for
danger or a potential meal.

Donkey skull

Brain case

Gavial skull

*Eye socket on
side of head*

FRONT VIEW
From the front,
only the eyes and
nostrils of this
crocodile are visible
above the water.

*Cheek muscles
attach here*

A LOT OF CHEEK
The donkey's long
mouth and large
cheeks accommodate
its powerful chewing
muscles. Like many
animals at risk from
attack by meat eaters,
the donkey has eyes on
the sides of its skull, to
keep an all-around
watch for danger.

Snowy owl with huge
eyes designed for
nocturnal
hunting

*Teeth running along
edge of upper jaw*

NIGHT VISION
An owl's eyes are so well
adapted for seeing in the dark
that they are too big to swivel within
their sockets in the skull. To look
sideways, the owl must turn its
head at the neck (p. 19).

*Long teeth at
tip of jaw*

Nostril at tip of snout

A donkey can move its long ears
in the direction of a sound

Nostrils

Jaws and feeding

THE SHAPE OF AN animal's jaws and teeth tells us what type of food it eats. Long, thin jaws with small teeth toward the front are good at probing and nibbling. These jaws are useful for eating small items such as berries or insects. But such a design does not have the crushing power of short, broad jaws, with large teeth near the back. This type of jaw is useful for grinding tough plant material or cracking bone and gristle. Many animals have a combination design: medium-length jaws with sharp teeth at the front for cutting and snipping, and flat teeth at the back for crushing and grinding.

Rodents

Mice, rats, squirrels, and coypus are rodents. They are herbivores, but their front four teeth are large and sharp - specially adapted for gnawing.

Large areas to anchor jaw and neck muscles for biting and pulling

Coypu skull

Orange enamel on incisors

Gap for sealing mouth

Coypu

NON-STOP GNAWING
A rodent's front teeth never stop growing, but they are worn down continually by use. The gap in the tooth row allows the lips to seal off the inside of the mouth when gnawing.

Lower jaw moves up and down

Herbivores

Cows, horses, camels, sheep, goats, and deer are herbivores - they have a diet of plants. The lower jawbone is generally deep at the back, giving a large area to anchor the strong chewing muscle. Special jaw joints allow sideways movement of the jaws as well as up-and-down chewing.

Goat skull

Deep lower jaw for muscle attachment

Goat

Lower jaw moves from side to side and back and forth

Position of horny pad

Molar and premolar grinders

Gap allows tongue to manipulate bulky food

PULLING OFF A MOUTHFUL
Like many herbivores, the goat has no top front teeth. It pulls at food using its tough tongue and lips, its padded upper gums and small lower incisors (missing from this specimen). Its jaws also slide front-to-back for even better grinding.

Position of lower incisors

Omnivores

These are animals that eat both plant and animal foods - anything from small, soft berries to gristly chunks of meat. To cope with the varied diet, their jaws and teeth are usually less specialized than those of carnivores or herbivores.

Chimpanzee

Chimpanzee skull

Limited sideways movement

Lower jaw moves up and down

Temporalis muscle attaches here

Deep flange for chewing muscle

Large canines

OUR CLOSEST RELATIVE
The chimp's jaws and teeth are similar to a human's, but larger in proportion to its skull. They mainly slice and chew, since the hands gather the food. The chimp's jaw joint is more rigid than a human's, so the animal cannot chew with as large a side-to-side movement as we can. Because of this its teeth are worn into a pattern of high points and cusps, in contrast to the more rounded human teeth.

Carnivores

Animals with jaws and teeth adapted solely to meat eating are known as carnivores, and include such animals as lions, tigers, cats, and dogs. Most of them have thick, heavy jaws for their size. The jaw-closing temporalis muscle runs from the rear of the lower jaw to the flange at the back of the skull, for a powerful bite even when the mouth is open wide.

Lion skull

Canines seize and tear prey

Lower jaw moves up and down only

Lion

SKULL OF THE KING
The lion has a massive cheek ridge of bone. The huge masseter muscle runs from here to the lower jaw, for crushing power when the mouth is almost closed. The fearsome front teeth have deep roots for strength as the prey struggles.

Masseter muscle attaches here

Carnassial teeth shear past each other to cut up meat

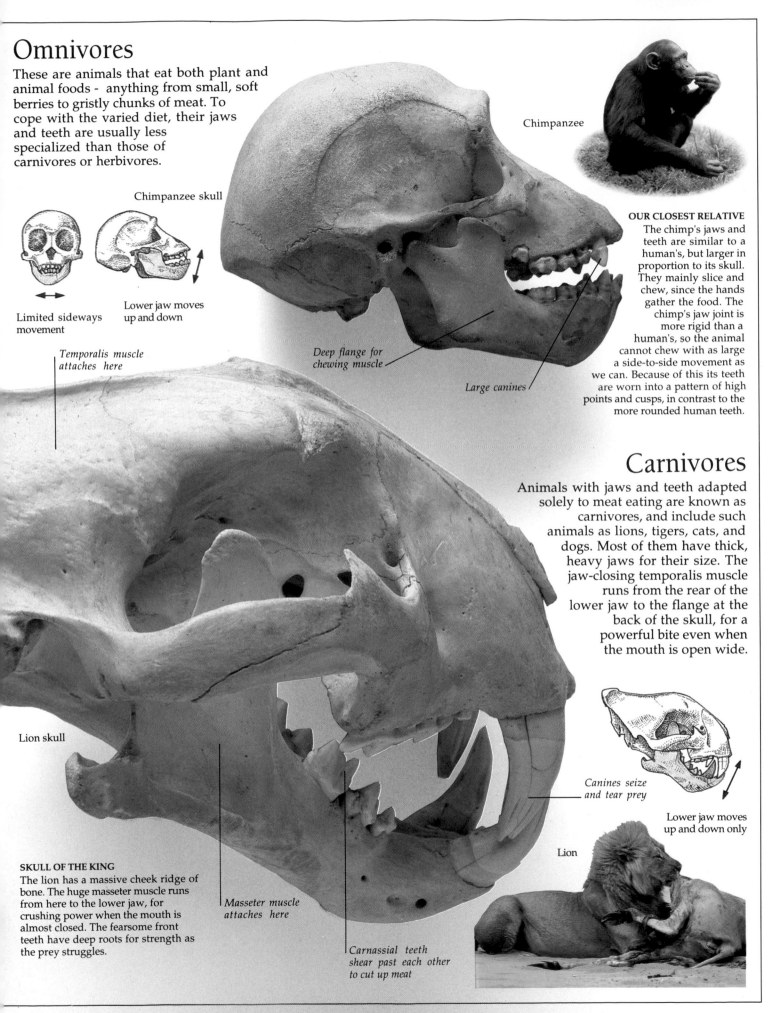

Animal teeth

BECAUSE OF THE NUMEROUS JOBS that animals' teeth are adapted to do, they vary widely in size and shape. Human teeth are relatively small and not particularly specialized we have cooking and knives and forks to help us. Animal teeth have to do many different jobs, from simple biting and slicing to chewing, crushing, and cracking, gnawing, grooming, digging, defending, and communicating. Teeth give many clues about their owner, from the type of food eaten to the age of the animal. The phrase "long in the tooth" refers to how the gums shrink in older animals and expose more of the tooth so it looks longer.

These leopards from Kenya were each made from the ivory of seven elephant tusks

The biggest teeth are elephant's tusks; the smallest, the teeth on a slug's tongue.

IVORY HUNTERS *above*
Countless elephants died for their ivory tusks. Ivory was used for white piano keys, billiard balls, and exotic carvings. The killing is now controlled, but poaching continues.

African elephant's molar tooth

MOVING MOLARS
Elephants have six molars on each side of the upper and lower jaws. These develop one by one and move forward in a conveyor-belt fashion. Only one or two teeth in each side of the jaw is in use at a time. When the last teeth have worn away, the animal can no longer eat. Ridges on the tooth improve its grinding efficiency.

Enamel ridge

Cement

Rear root

Dentine between ridges

Front root

Herbivores and carnivores

Herbivores, like horses and zebras (p. 34), must chew their food well before they swallow it, since unchewed plant material is difficult to digest chemically in the stomach and intestine. Their cheek teeth (molars) are broad and flat. Carnivores, animals that eat only meat (p. 35), have more pointed teeth for catching and slicing; less chewing is needed as meat is easier to digest.

Lower jawbone of horse

Incisors for grass cutting

Jawbone cut away to show long roots

Dog's teeth

Molars

Broad surface for chewing

above. **LONG-CROWNED MOLARS**
The horse's incisor teeth, at the front, grip and pull off mouthfuls of grass. The huge molars and premolars pulverize the food to a pulp. They are deeply anchored in the jaws, as can be seen above in the cutaway part of the horse's lower jawbone.

TEETH FOR TEARING AND SLICING
This selection of teeth from a dog's upper jaw shows carnivorous features. Each type of tooth has a special function and so assumes its particular shape.

Bone-cracking molar

Cutting carnassial

Crushing premolar

Long stabbing canine

Small gripping incisor

36

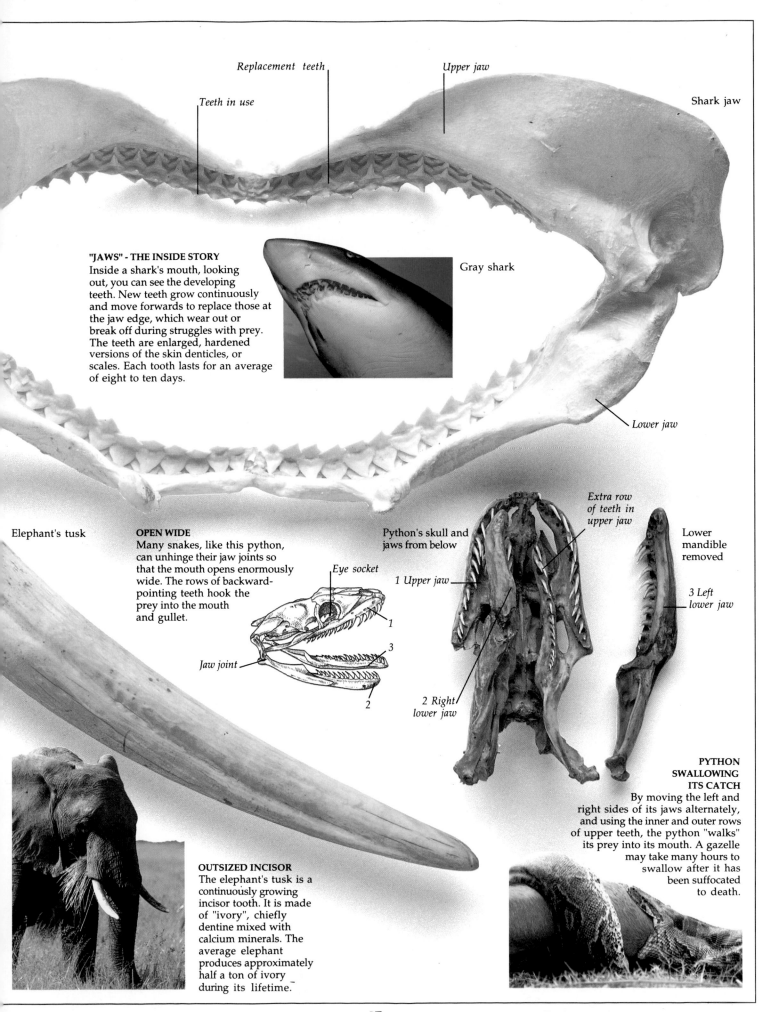

Replacement teeth

Teeth in use

Upper jaw

Shark jaw

"JAWS" - THE INSIDE STORY
Inside a shark's mouth, looking out, you can see the developing teeth. New teeth grow continuously and move forwards to replace those at the jaw edge, which wear out or break off during struggles with prey. The teeth are enlarged, hardened versions of the skin denticles, or scales. Each tooth lasts for an average of eight to ten days.

Gray shark

Lower jaw

Elephant's tusk

OPEN WIDE
Many snakes, like this python, can unhinge their jaw joints so that the mouth opens enormously wide. The rows of backward-pointing teeth hook the prey into the mouth and gullet.

Eye socket

Jaw joint

1

3

2

Python's skull and jaws from below

Extra row of teeth in upper jaw

Lower mandible removed

1 Upper jaw

3 Left lower jaw

2 Right lower jaw

PYTHON SWALLOWING ITS CATCH
By moving the left and right sides of its jaws alternately, and using the inner and outer rows of upper teeth, the python "walks" its prey into its mouth. A gazelle may take many hours to swallow after it has been suffocated to death.

OUTSIZED INCISOR
The elephant's tusk is a continuously growing incisor tooth. It is made of "ivory", chiefly dentine mixed with calcium minerals. The average elephant produces approximately half a ton of ivory during its lifetime.

The human spine

T HE SPINE is literally the "back bone" of the human body. It forms a vertical supporting rod for the head, arms, and legs. It allows us to stoop and squat, to turn and nod the head, and to twist the shoulders and hips. Yet it was originally designed as a horizontal girder, to take the weight of the chest and abdomen: the original prehistoric mammals almost certainly moved on all fours (p. 46). In the upright human, the spine has an S-shaped curve when seen from the side, to balance the various parts of the body over the legs and feet and reduce muscle strain when standing. The human spine works on the chain-link principle: many small movements add up. Each vertebra can only move a little in relation to its neighbors. But over the whole row this means the back can bend double. The spine shown below is "lying on its side", with the head end to the left and the "tail" on the right.

This engraving, from an anatomy book of 1685, features a back view of the human skeleton

THE CURVED SPINE *above*
From the side, the spine has a slight S-shape. This helps to bring the centers of gravity of the head, arms, chest and abdomen above the legs, so that the body as a whole is well balanced.

BELOW THE SKULL
The first two vertebrae are called the atlas and the axis. All of the upper spine contributes to head movements, but these top two vertebrae are specialized to allow the head to nod and twist.

Atlas allows nodding movements

Axis allows side to side movements

IN THE NECK
There are seven vertebrae in the neck, called the cervical vertebrae. They allow us to turn our head in roughly three-quarters of a circle without moving the shoulders. (By moving our eyes as well, we can see in a complete circle.) Muscles run from the "wings" (transverse processes and neural spine) on the sides and rear of each vertebra to the skull, shoulder blades, and lower vertebrae. This steadies the head on the neck.

Cervical vertebra from behind

IN THE CHEST
The vertebrae become larger the lower they are in the spine, since they have to carry increasing weight. There are 12 chest (or thoracic) vertebrae, one for each pair of ribs. The ribs join to shallow cups on the body of the vertebra. The upper 10 pairs of ribs also join to hollows on the transverse processes for extra stability. These two sets of joints move slightly every time you breathe.

Thoracic vertebra from behind

Shallow socket for end of rib

Body (centrum) of vertebra

Transverse process

Neural canal - hole for spinal cord

Cervical vertebra from top

Neural arch

Neural spine

Transverse process

Thoracic vertebra from top

Neural spine

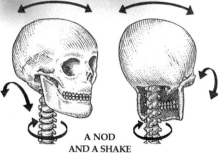
A NOD AND A SHAKE
The topmost vertebra, the atlas, allows nodding movements of the head. Side to side movements are a result of the atlas swiveling on the axis.

The protective role of the spine

The large holes in each vertebra line up to form a bony tunnel or canal. Inside this, well protected from knocks and twists, is the delicate spinal cord. Nerves enter and leave the cord through gaps between neighboring vertebrae. Occasionally, a disc of cartilage between two vertebrae is squashed and presses on the nerve, causing the pain of a "slipped disc."

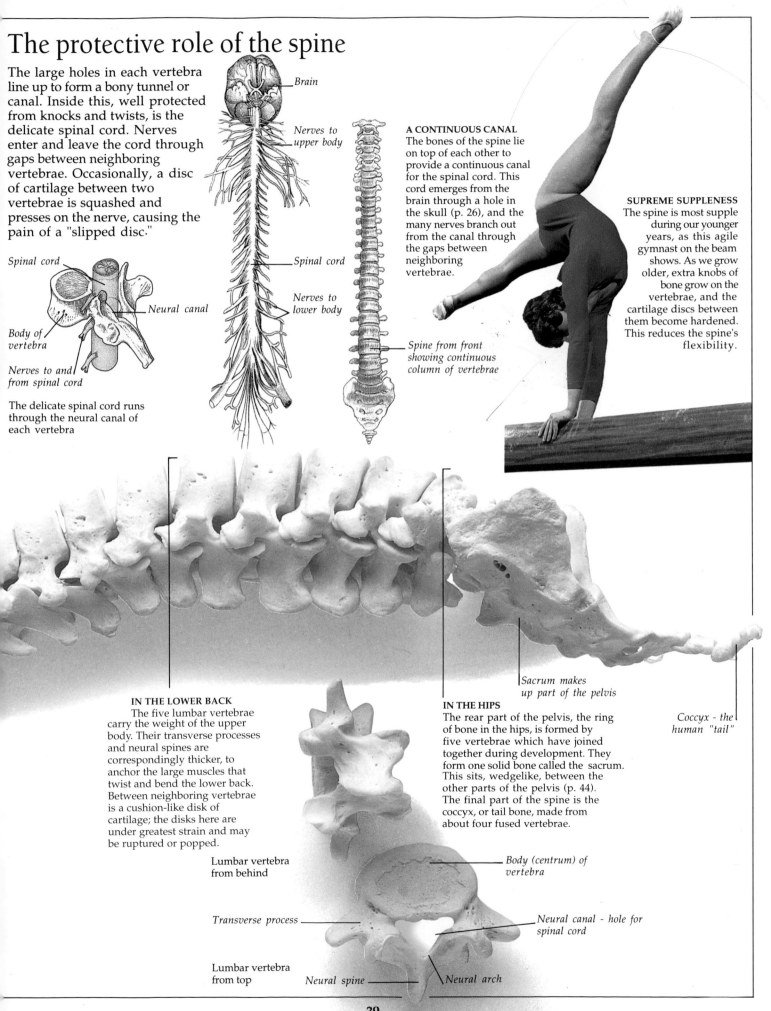

Spinal cord

Neural canal

Body of vertebra

Nerves to and from spinal cord

The delicate spinal cord runs through the neural canal of each vertebra

Brain

Nerves to upper body

Spinal cord

Nerves to lower body

Spine from front showing continuous column of vertebrae

A CONTINUOUS CANAL
The bones of the spine lie on top of each other to provide a continuous canal for the spinal cord. This cord emerges from the brain through a hole in the skull (p. 26), and the many nerves branch out from the canal through the gaps between neighboring vertebrae.

SUPREME SUPPLENESS
The spine is most supple during our younger years, as this agile gymnast on the beam shows. As we grow older, extra knobs of bone grow on the vertebrae, and the cartilage discs between them become hardened. This reduces the spine's flexibility.

IN THE LOWER BACK
The five lumbar vertebrae carry the weight of the upper body. Their transverse processes and neural spines are correspondingly thicker, to anchor the large muscles that twist and bend the lower back. Between neighboring vertebrae is a cushion-like disk of cartilage; the disks here are under greatest strain and may be ruptured or popped.

Lumbar vertebra from behind

Transverse process

Lumbar vertebra from top

Neural spine

Neural arch

Sacrum makes up part of the pelvis

IN THE HIPS
The rear part of the pelvis, the ring of bone in the hips, is formed by five vertebrae which have joined together during development. They form one solid bone called the sacrum. This sits, wedgelike, between the other parts of the pelvis (p. 44). The final part of the spine is the coccyx, or tail bone, made from about four fused vertebrae.

Coccyx - the human "tail"

Body (centrum) of vertebra

Neural canal - hole for spinal cord

Animal backbones

Every fish, reptile, amphibian, bird, and mammal has a row of bones in its back, usually called the spine or spinal column. This is the feature that groups them together as vertebrates (animals with backbones or vertebrae), distinguishing them from invertebrates such as insects and worms (p. 22). The basic spine design is a row of small bones, linked together into a flexible column, with the skull at one end and a tail (usually) at the other. However, the number of individual vertebrae varies from as few as nine in a frog to more than 400 in some snakes!

A GRIPPING TAIL
The end of the lemur's spine - its tail - is prehensile and serves as a fifth limb, to grip branches while climbing. This also leaves both hands free when feeding.

Ring-tailed lemurs

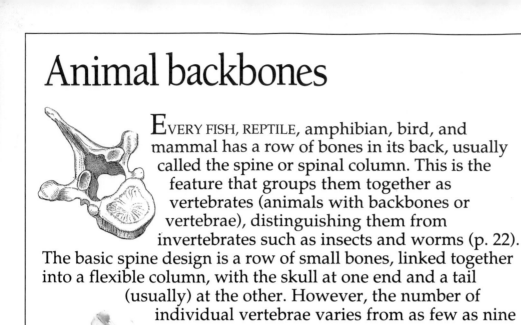

Nose to tail length - 35 in (89 cm)

First two vertebrae allow head to twist and nod

HEAD TO TAIL
A fox has about 50 vertebrae; about half of these are in its "brush" or tail. Those in the hip region have large flanges (ridges) for the muscles and ligaments that secure the pelvis.

Red fox

Region of stomach

SLITHERING ALONG
In a snake each vertebra, with its pair of ribs, is virtually identical to all the others. A snake's skeleton is all backbone as it has no arms, legs, shoulder blades, or pelvis. Large snakes, such as this python, use their belly scales to move. The scales, attached to the ribs, are pushed backwards in groups; their rear edges are tilted down to grip the ground.

Shoulder blades linked here

Python skeleton

Reticulated python

Region of heart

Skull

Lower jaw

AGILE REPTILES
Lack of limbs does not seem to restrict snakes, such as this reticulated python. They can move very fast, climb, swim, and burrow.

Region of intestine

Rib

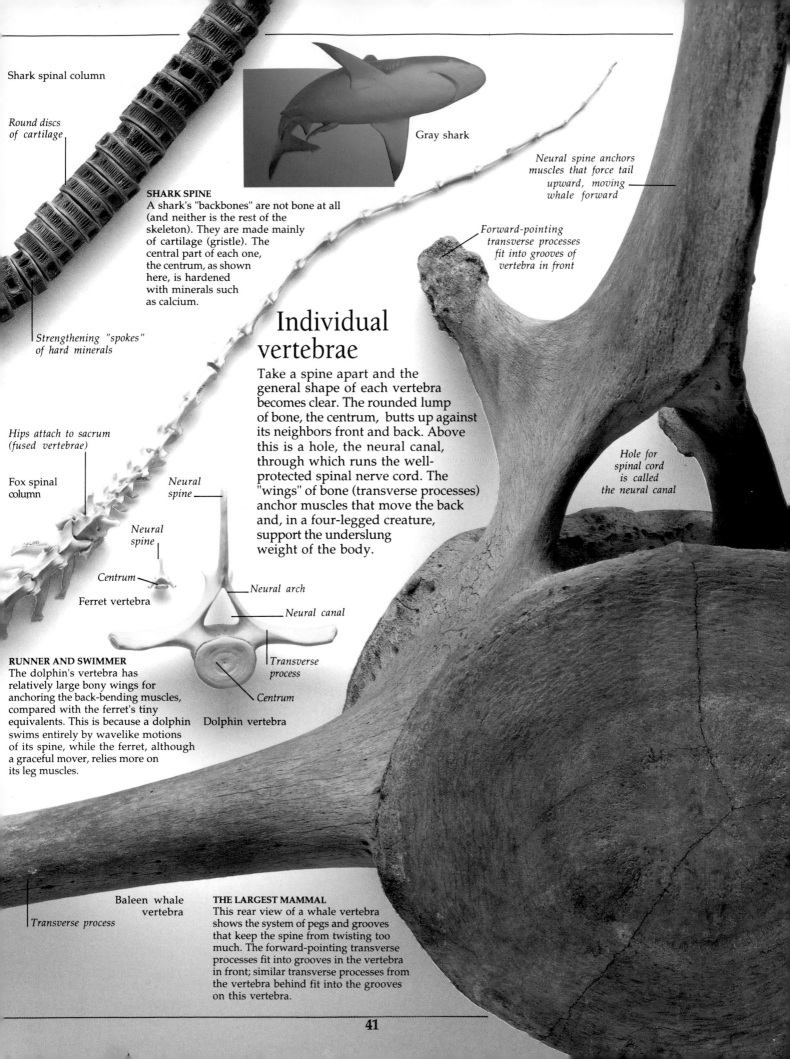

Shark spinal column

Round discs of cartilage

Gray shark

SHARK SPINE
A shark's "backbones" are not bone at all (and neither is the rest of the skeleton). They are made mainly of cartilage (gristle). The central part of each one, the centrum, as shown here, is hardened with minerals such as calcium.

Strengthening "spokes" of hard minerals

Neural spine anchors muscles that force tail upward, moving whale forward

Forward-pointing transverse processes fit into grooves of vertebra in front

Individual vertebrae

Take a spine apart and the general shape of each vertebra becomes clear. The rounded lump of bone, the centrum, butts up against its neighbors front and back. Above this is a hole, the neural canal, through which runs the well-protected spinal nerve cord. The "wings" of bone (transverse processes) anchor muscles that move the back and, in a four-legged creature, support the underslung weight of the body.

Hips attach to sacrum (fused vertebrae)

Fox spinal column

Neural spine

Neural spine

Hole for spinal cord is called the neural canal

Centrum

Ferret vertebra

Neural arch

Neural canal

Transverse process

RUNNER AND SWIMMER
The dolphin's vertebra has relatively large bony wings for anchoring the back-bending muscles, compared with the ferret's tiny equivalents. This is because a dolphin swims entirely by wavelike motions of its spine, while the ferret, although a graceful mover, relies more on its leg muscles.

Centrum

Dolphin vertebra

Baleen whale vertebra

Transverse process

THE LARGEST MAMMAL
This rear view of a whale vertebra shows the system of pegs and grooves that keep the spine from twisting too much. The forward-pointing transverse processes fit into grooves in the vertebra in front; similar transverse processes from the vertebra behind fit into the grooves on this vertebra.

The rib cage

Problem: the lungs need to inflate and deflate, becoming larger and smaller as they breathe; yet they also need protection against being knocked or crushed. A solid case of protective bone, like the skull around the brain, would be too rigid. Answer: a flexible cage with movable bars - the ribs. Closely spaced, with tough ligaments and muscles between them, the ribs give good protection to the delicate lungs. In addition, each rib is thin and flexible, so that it can absorb knocks without cracking and puncturing the vital airtight seal around the lungs. The ribs move at the points where they join the spine and breastbone. When breathing in, muscles lift the ribs upwards and swing them outward, increasing the volume of the chest and sucking air into the lungs.

Inside the chest

The ribs protect the lungs and also the other organs in the chest, such as the heart and main blood vessels. And they guard the stomach, liver, and other parts of the upper abdomen. These organs nestle under the diaphragm, a dome-shaped muscle that forms the base of the chest, so they are above the level of the bottom ribs.

The depth of the rib cage and its relation to the spine is shown in this sideways view by Leonardo da Vinci (1452-1519)

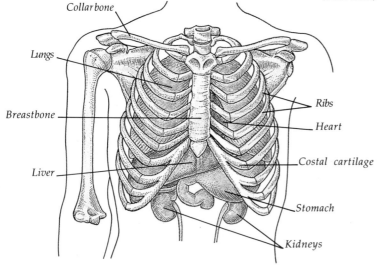

Collarbone

Lungs

Breastbone

Liver

Ribs

Heart

Costal cartilage

Stomach

Kidneys

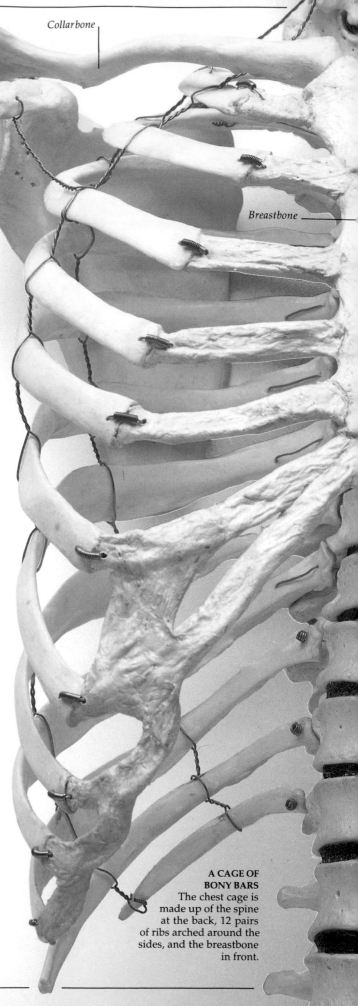

Collarbone

Breastbone

A CAGE OF BONY BARS
The chest cage is made up of the spine at the back, 12 pairs of ribs arched around the sides, and the breastbone in front.

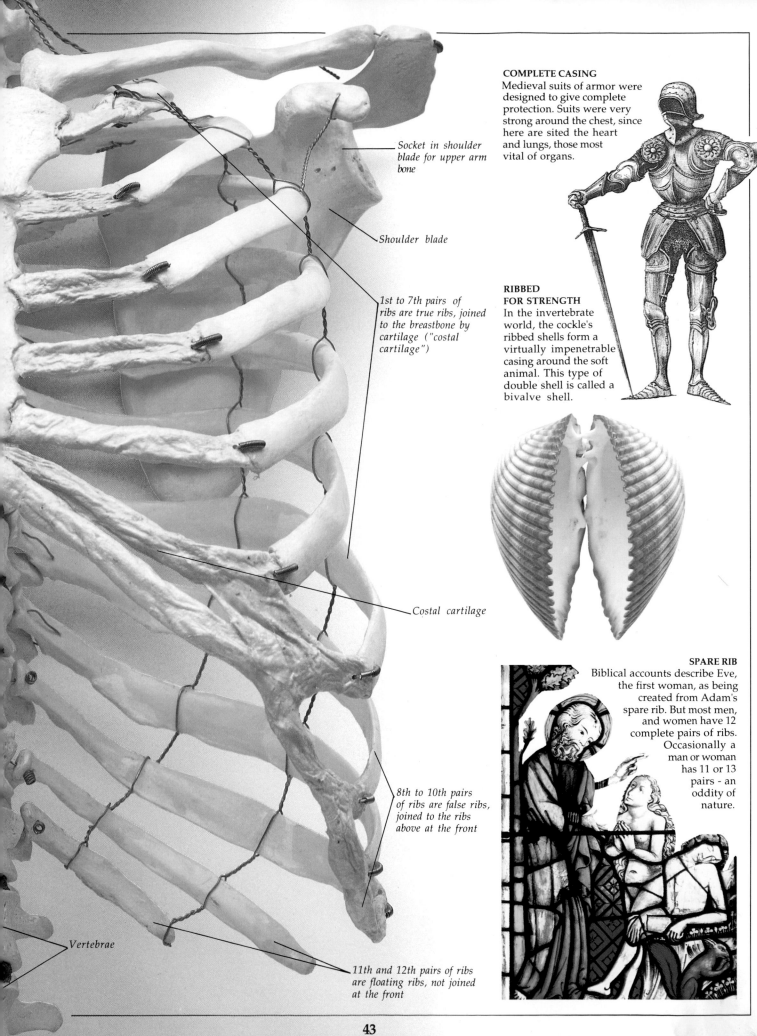

Socket in shoulder
blade for upper arm
bone

Shoulder blade

1st to 7th pairs of
ribs are true ribs, joined
to the breastbone by
cartilage ("costal
cartilage")

Costal cartilage

8th to 10th pairs
of ribs are false ribs,
joined to the ribs
above at the front

Vertebrae

11th and 12th pairs of ribs
are floating ribs, not joined
at the front

COMPLETE CASING
Medieval suits of armor were
designed to give complete
protection. Suits were very
strong around the chest, since
here are sited the heart
and lungs, those most
vital of organs.

**RIBBED
FOR STRENGTH**
In the invertebrate
world, the cockle's
ribbed shells form a
virtually impenetrable
casing around the soft
animal. This type of
double shell is called a
bivalve shell.

SPARE RIB
Biblical accounts describe Eve,
the first woman, as being
created from Adam's
spare rib. But most men,
and women have 12
complete pairs of ribs.
Occasionally a
man or woman
has 11 or 13
pairs - an
oddity of
nature.

Human hip bones

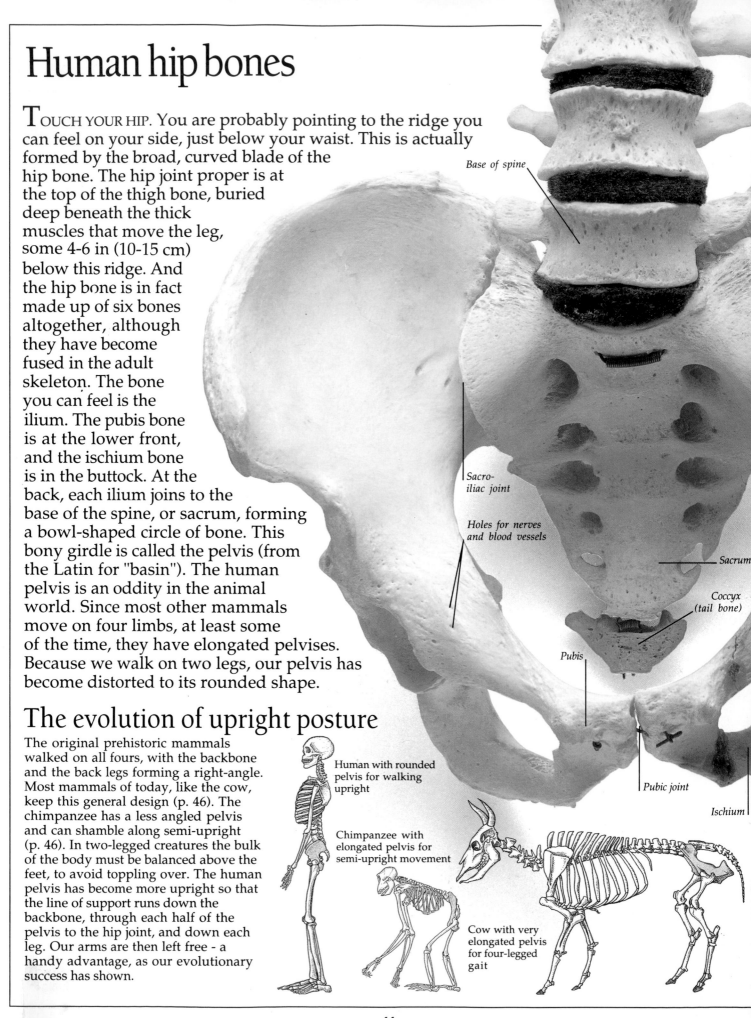

TOUCH YOUR HIP. You are probably pointing to the ridge you can feel on your side, just below your waist. This is actually formed by the broad, curved blade of the hip bone. The hip joint proper is at the top of the thigh bone, buried deep beneath the thick muscles that move the leg, some 4-6 in (10-15 cm) below this ridge. And the hip bone is in fact made up of six bones altogether, although they have become fused in the adult skeleton. The bone you can feel is the ilium. The pubis bone is at the lower front, and the ischium bone is in the buttock. At the back, each ilium joins to the base of the spine, or sacrum, forming a bowl-shaped circle of bone. This bony girdle is called the pelvis (from the Latin for "basin"). The human pelvis is an oddity in the animal world. Since most other mammals move on four limbs, at least some of the time, they have elongated pelvises. Because we walk on two legs, our pelvis has become distorted to its rounded shape.

Base of spine

Sacro-iliac joint

Holes for nerves and blood vessels

Sacrum

Coccyx (tail bone)

Pubis

Pubic joint

Ischium

The evolution of upright posture

The original prehistoric mammals walked on all fours, with the backbone and the back legs forming a right-angle. Most mammals of today, like the cow, keep this general design (p. 46). The chimpanzee has a less angled pelvis and can shamble along semi-upright (p. 46). In two-legged creatures the bulk of the body must be balanced above the feet, to avoid toppling over. The human pelvis has become more upright so that the line of support runs down the backbone, through each half of the pelvis to the hip joint, and down each leg. Our arms are then left free - a handy advantage, as our evolutionary success has shown.

Human with rounded pelvis for walking upright

Chimpanzee with elongated pelvis for semi-upright movement

Cow with very elongated pelvis for four-legged gait

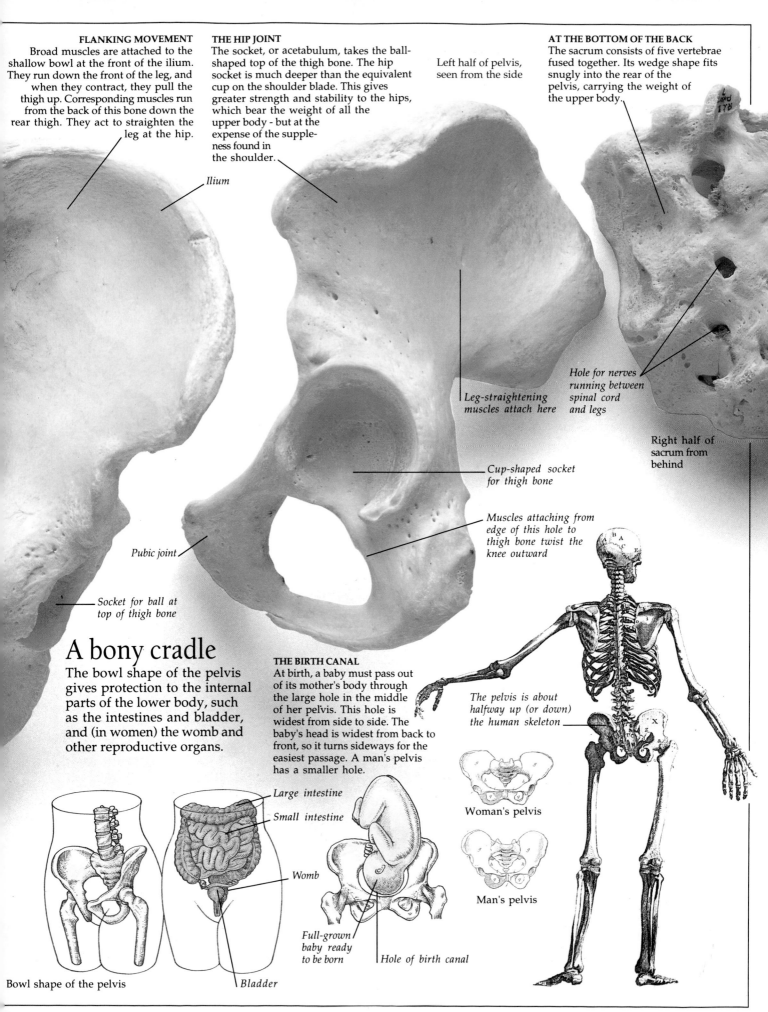

FLANKING MOVEMENT
Broad muscles are attached to the shallow bowl at the front of the ilium. They run down the front of the leg, and when they contract, they pull the thigh up. Corresponding muscles run from the back of this bone down the rear thigh. They act to straighten the leg at the hip.

Ilium

THE HIP JOINT
The socket, or acetabulum, takes the ball-shaped top of the thigh bone. The hip socket is much deeper than the equivalent cup on the shoulder blade. This gives greater strength and stability to the hips, which bear the weight of all the upper body - but at the expense of the suppleness found in the shoulder.

Left half of pelvis, seen from the side

AT THE BOTTOM OF THE BACK
The sacrum consists of five vertebrae fused together. Its wedge shape fits snugly into the rear of the pelvis, carrying the weight of the upper body.

Leg-straightening muscles attach here

Hole for nerves running between spinal cord and legs

Right half of sacrum from behind

Cup-shaped socket for thigh bone

Muscles attaching from edge of this hole to thigh bone twist the knee outward

Pubic joint

Socket for ball at top of thigh bone

A bony cradle
The bowl shape of the pelvis gives protection to the internal parts of the lower body, such as the intestines and bladder, and (in women) the womb and other reproductive organs.

THE BIRTH CANAL
At birth, a baby must pass out of its mother's body through the large hole in the middle of her pelvis. This hole is widest from side to side. The baby's head is widest from back to front, so it turns sideways for the easiest passage. A man's pelvis has a smaller hole.

The pelvis is about halfway up (or down) the human skeleton

Large intestine

Small intestine

Womb

Woman's pelvis

Man's pelvis

Full-grown baby ready to be born

Hole of birth canal

Bowl shape of the pelvis

Bladder

45

Animal hip bones

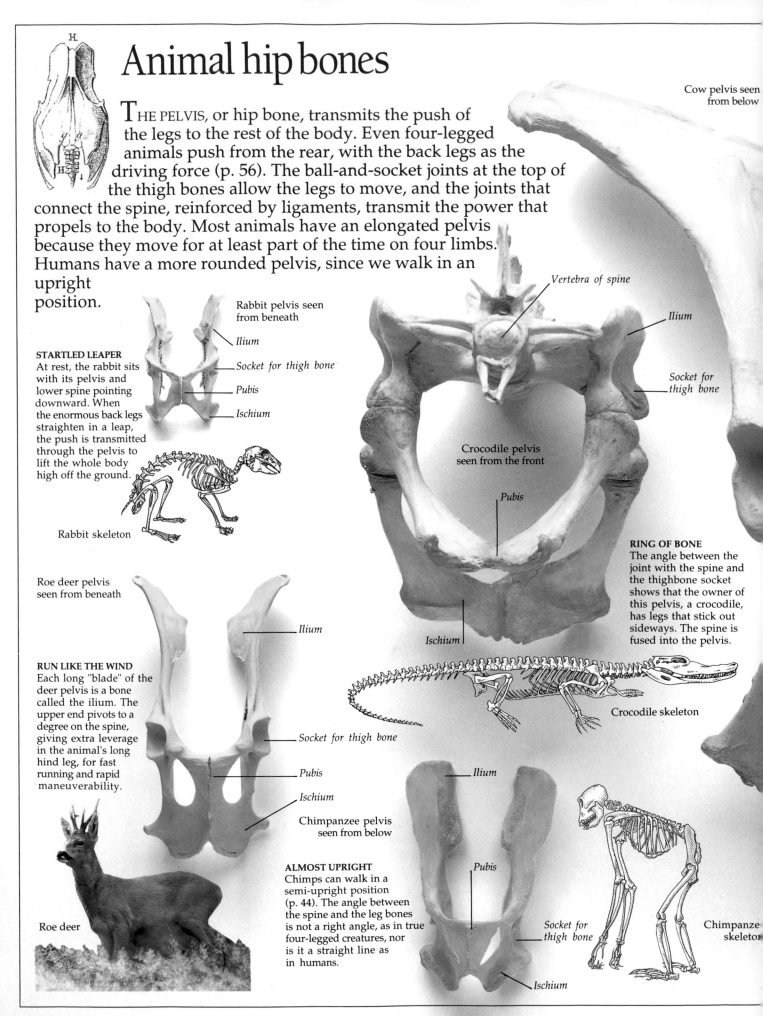

THE PELVIS, or hip bone, transmits the push of the legs to the rest of the body. Even four-legged animals push from the rear, with the back legs as the driving force (p. 56). The ball-and-socket joints at the top of the thigh bones allow the legs to move, and the joints that connect the spine, reinforced by ligaments, transmit the power that propels to the body. Most animals have an elongated pelvis because they move for at least part of the time on four limbs. Humans have a more rounded pelvis, since we walk in an upright position.

Cow pelvis seen from below

Rabbit pelvis seen from beneath

Ilium
Socket for thigh bone
Pubis
Ischium

STARTLED LEAPER
At rest, the rabbit sits with its pelvis and lower spine pointing downward. When the enormous back legs straighten in a leap, the push is transmitted through the pelvis to lift the whole body high off the ground.

Rabbit skeleton

Vertebra of spine

Ilium

Socket for thigh bone

Crocodile pelvis seen from the front

Pubis

Ischium

RING OF BONE
The angle between the joint with the spine and the thighbone socket shows that the owner of this pelvis, a crocodile, has legs that stick out sideways. The spine is fused into the pelvis.

Roe deer pelvis seen from beneath

Ilium

RUN LIKE THE WIND
Each long "blade" of the deer pelvis is a bone called the ilium. The upper end pivots to a degree on the spine, giving extra leverage in the animal's long hind leg, for fast running and rapid maneuverability.

Socket for thigh bone

Pubis

Ischium

Crocodile skeleton

Chimpanzee pelvis seen from below

Ilium

Pubis

ALMOST UPRIGHT
Chimps can walk in a semi-upright position (p. 44). The angle between the spine and the leg bones is not a right angle, as in true four-legged creatures, nor is it a straight line as in humans.

Socket for thigh bone

Chimpanzee skeleton

Ischium

Roe deer

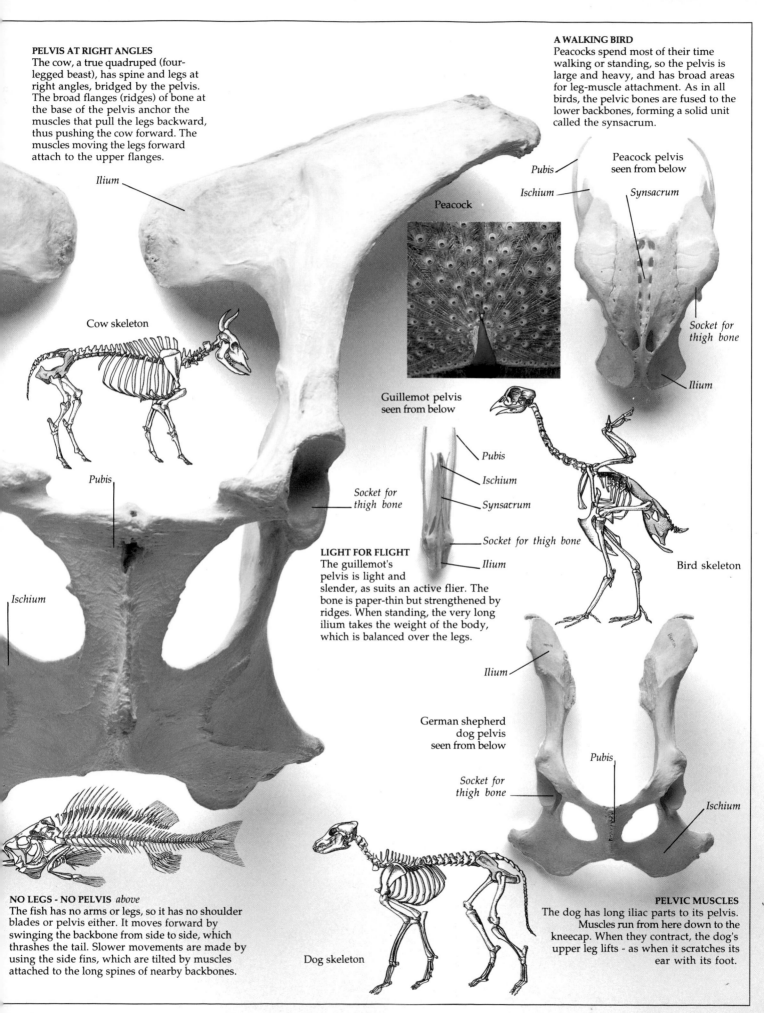

PELVIS AT RIGHT ANGLES
The cow, a true quadruped (four-legged beast), has spine and legs at right angles, bridged by the pelvis. The broad flanges (ridges) of bone at the base of the pelvis anchor the muscles that pull the legs backward, thus pushing the cow forward. The muscles moving the legs forward attach to the upper flanges.

Ilium

Cow skeleton

Pubis

Ischium

A WALKING BIRD
Peacocks spend most of their time walking or standing, so the pelvis is large and heavy, and has broad areas for leg-muscle attachment. As in all birds, the pelvic bones are fused to the lower backbones, forming a solid unit called the synsacrum.

Pubis

Peacock pelvis seen from below

Ischium

Synsacrum

Peacock

Socket for thigh bone

Ilium

Guillemot pelvis seen from below

Socket for thigh bone

Pubis

Ischium

Synsacrum

Socket for thigh bone

Ilium

LIGHT FOR FLIGHT
The guillemot's pelvis is light and slender, as suits an active flier. The bone is paper-thin but strengthened by ridges. When standing, the very long ilium takes the weight of the body, which is balanced over the legs.

Bird skeleton

Ilium

German shepherd dog pelvis seen from below

Socket for thigh bone

Pubis

Ischium

NO LEGS - NO PELVIS *above*
The fish has no arms or legs, so it has no shoulder blades or pelvis either. It moves forward by swinging the backbone from side to side, which thrashes the tail. Slower movements are made by using the side fins, which are tilted by muscles attached to the long spines of nearby backbones.

Dog skeleton

PELVIC MUSCLES
The dog has long iliac parts to its pelvis. Muscles run from here down to the kneecap. When they contract, the dog's upper leg lifts - as when it scratches its ear with its foot.

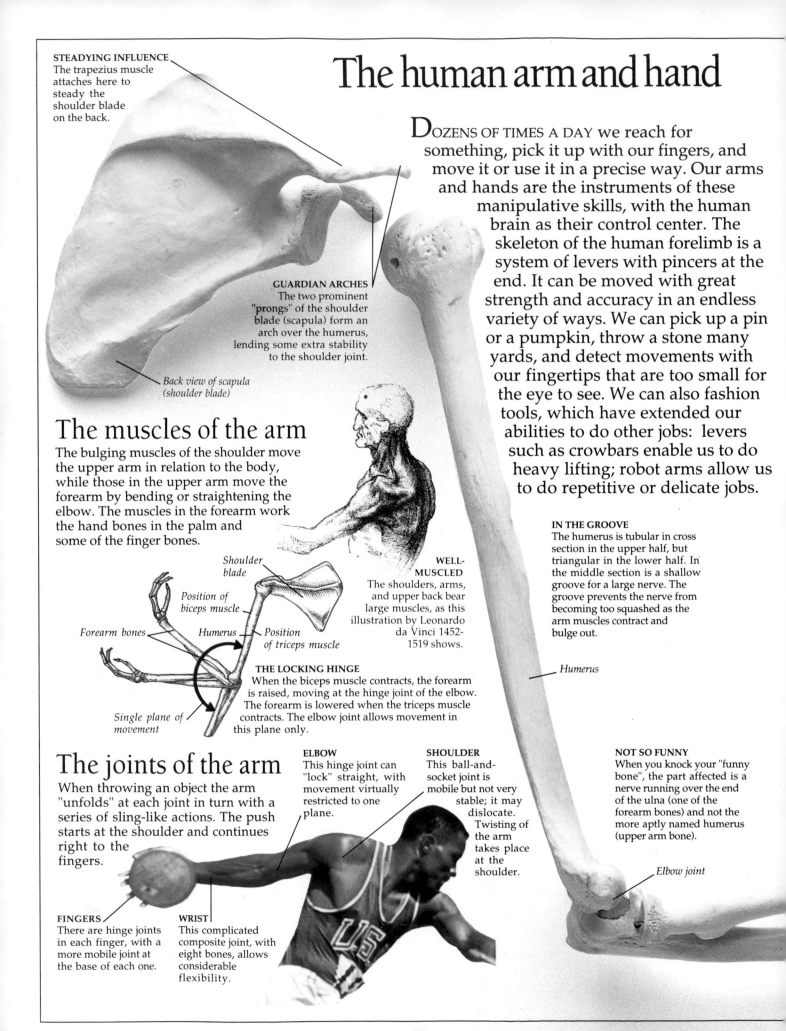

STEADYING INFLUENCE
The trapezius muscle attaches here to steady the shoulder blade on the back.

GUARDIAN ARCHES
The two prominent "prongs" of the shoulder blade (scapula) form an arch over the humerus, lending some extra stability to the shoulder joint.

Back view of scapula (shoulder blade)

D OZENS OF TIMES A DAY we reach for something, pick it up with our fingers, and move it or use it in a precise way. Our arms and hands are the instruments of these manipulative skills, with the human brain as their control center. The skeleton of the human forelimb is a system of levers with pincers at the end. It can be moved with great strength and accuracy in an endless variety of ways. We can pick up a pin or a pumpkin, throw a stone many yards, and detect movements with our fingertips that are too small for the eye to see. We can also fashion tools, which have extended our abilities to do other jobs: levers such as crowbars enable us to do heavy lifting; robot arms allow us to do repetitive or delicate jobs.

The muscles of the arm

The bulging muscles of the shoulder move the upper arm in relation to the body, while those in the upper arm move the forearm by bending or straightening the elbow. The muscles in the forearm work the hand bones in the palm and some of the finger bones.

Shoulder blade

Position of biceps muscle

Forearm bones

Humerus

Position of triceps muscle

Single plane of movement

WELL-MUSCLED
The shoulders, arms, and upper back bear large muscles, as this illustration by Leonardo da Vinci 1452-1519 shows.

THE LOCKING HINGE
When the biceps muscle contracts, the forearm is raised, moving at the hinge joint of the elbow. The forearm is lowered when the triceps muscle contracts. The elbow joint allows movement in this plane only.

IN THE GROOVE
The humerus is tubular in cross section in the upper half, but triangular in the lower half. In the middle section is a shallow groove for a large nerve. The groove prevents the nerve from becoming too squashed as the arm muscles contract and bulge out.

Humerus

The joints of the arm

When throwing an object the arm "unfolds" at each joint in turn with a series of sling-like actions. The push starts at the shoulder and continues right to the fingers.

ELBOW
This hinge joint can "lock" straight, with movement virtually restricted to one plane.

SHOULDER
This ball-and-socket joint is mobile but not very stable; it may dislocate. Twisting of the arm takes place at the shoulder.

NOT SO FUNNY
When you knock your "funny bone", the part affected is a nerve running over the end of the ulna (one of the forearm bones) and not the more aptly named humerus (upper arm bone).

Elbow joint

FINGERS
There are hinge joints in each finger, with a more mobile joint at the base of each one.

WRIST
This complicated composite joint, with eight bones, allows considerable flexibility.

The bones of the hand

Our hands are built on the standard mammal five-digit plan. Why the "magic number" should be five is not really known. The wrist bones provide anchorage for the small muscles that help to move the thumb and fingers. Other finger-moving muscles are in the forearm, connected to the fingers by long tendons that run through a "collar" of ligaments in the wrist.

Middle finger (3rd digit)

Index finger (2nd digit)

Ring finger (4th digit)

Little finger (5th digit)

Thumb (1st digit)

THE WRIST REVEALED
A computer-colored x-ray shows the wrist bones. Made of cartilage in babies, these turn to bone in a regular sequence during childhood. So wrist x-rays, which distinguish bone from cartilage, can be used to determine age.

PRECISION GRIP
The thumb can touch each fingertip in turn, as shown in this x-ray. This precision or "pincer" grip is the basis of the human hand's dexterity. Our close relatives, like the chimp, do not have such a long and mobile thumb (below) and lack the precision grip.

Main knuckle at base of each finger formed by ball-shaped head of bone

Chimp's hand showing position of less mobile thumb

Human's hand showing position of very mobile thumb

Wrist bones (carpals)

Radius and ulna join here

THUMB'S UP
The long metacarpal bones of the thumb are "hidden" in the palm of the hand. At the base of the first metacarpal is a very mobile "saddle" joint which allows the thumb to bend in two planes.

TWIST OF THE WRIST
Besides moving in relation to the humerus, to bend the elbow, the two forearm bones, the radius and ulna, also move on each other, at their upper and lower ends. They rotate to swivel over each other in a movement that twists the wrist.

Saddle joint

Wrist bones (carpals)

Radius

Ulna

ARM TO HAND
The eight wrist bones are wrapped in strong supporting ligaments. Each bone moves on all its neighbors.

Hand bones (metacarpals)

Finger bones (phalanges)

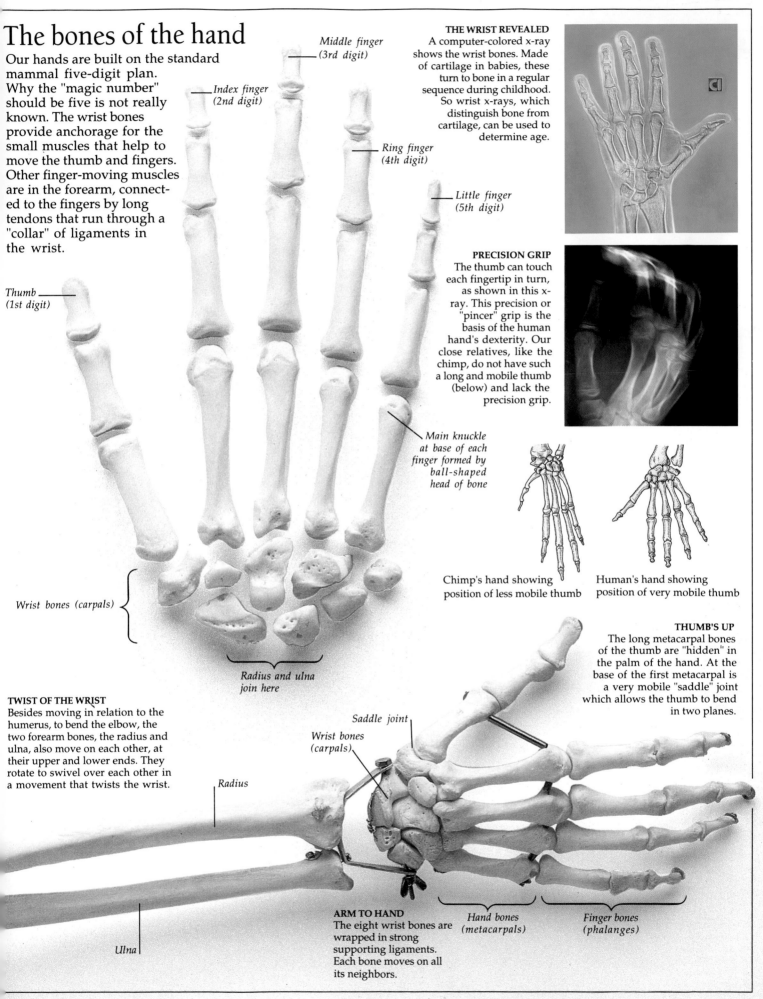

Arms, wings, and flippers

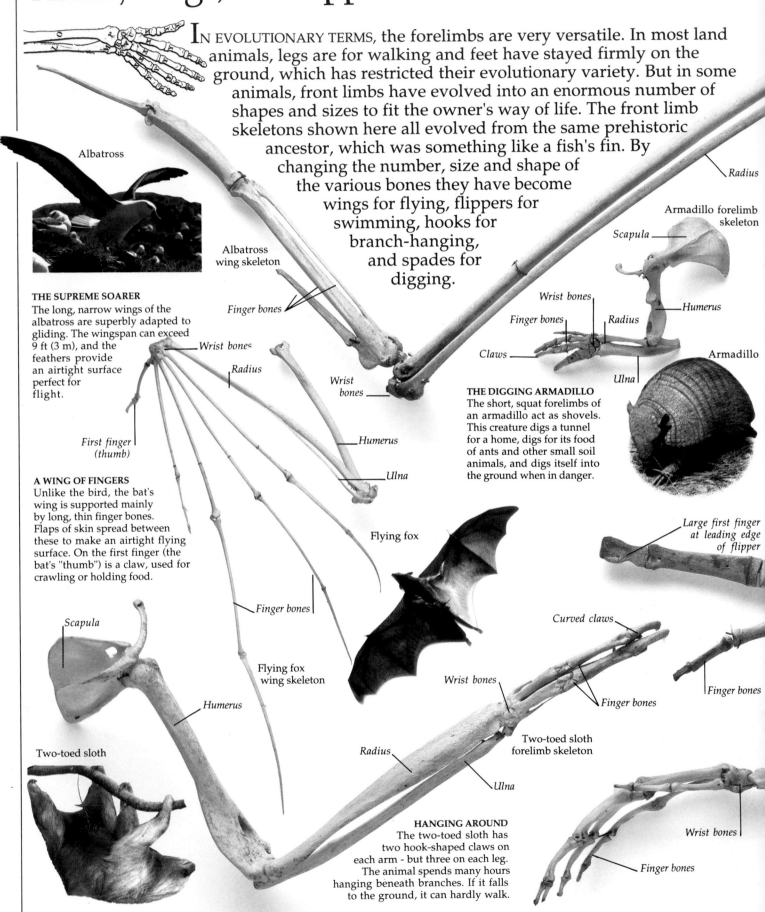

IN EVOLUTIONARY TERMS, the forelimbs are very versatile. In most land animals, legs are for walking and feet have stayed firmly on the ground, which has restricted their evolutionary variety. But in some animals, front limbs have evolved into an enormous number of shapes and sizes to fit the owner's way of life. The front limb skeletons shown here all evolved from the same prehistoric ancestor, which was something like a fish's fin. By changing the number, size and shape of the various bones they have become wings for flying, flippers for swimming, hooks for branch-hanging, and spades for digging.

Albatross

Albatross wing skeleton

Finger bones

THE SUPREME SOARER
The long, narrow wings of the albatross are superbly adapted to gliding. The wingspan can exceed 9 ft (3 m), and the feathers provide an airtight surface perfect for flight.

Wrist bones

Radius

First finger (thumb)

Wrist bones

Radius

Wrist bones

Humerus

Ulna

A WING OF FINGERS
Unlike the bird, the bat's wing is supported mainly by long, thin finger bones. Flaps of skin spread between these to make an airtight flying surface. On the first finger (the bat's "thumb") is a claw, used for crawling or holding food.

Radius

Armadillo forelimb skeleton

Scapula

Wrist bones

Finger bones

Radius

Claws

Humerus

Ulna

Armadillo

THE DIGGING ARMADILLO
The short, squat forelimbs of an armadillo act as shovels. This creature digs a tunnel for a home, digs for its food of ants and other small soil animals, and digs itself into the ground when in danger.

Flying fox

Large first finger at leading edge of flipper

Scapula

Finger bones

Flying fox wing skeleton

Humerus

Two-toed sloth

Curved claws

Wrist bones

Finger bones

Finger bones

Two-toed sloth forelimb skeleton

Radius

Ulna

HANGING AROUND
The two-toed sloth has two hook-shaped claws on each arm - but three on each leg. The animal spends many hours hanging beneath branches. If it falls to the ground, it can hardly walk.

Wrist bones

Finger bones

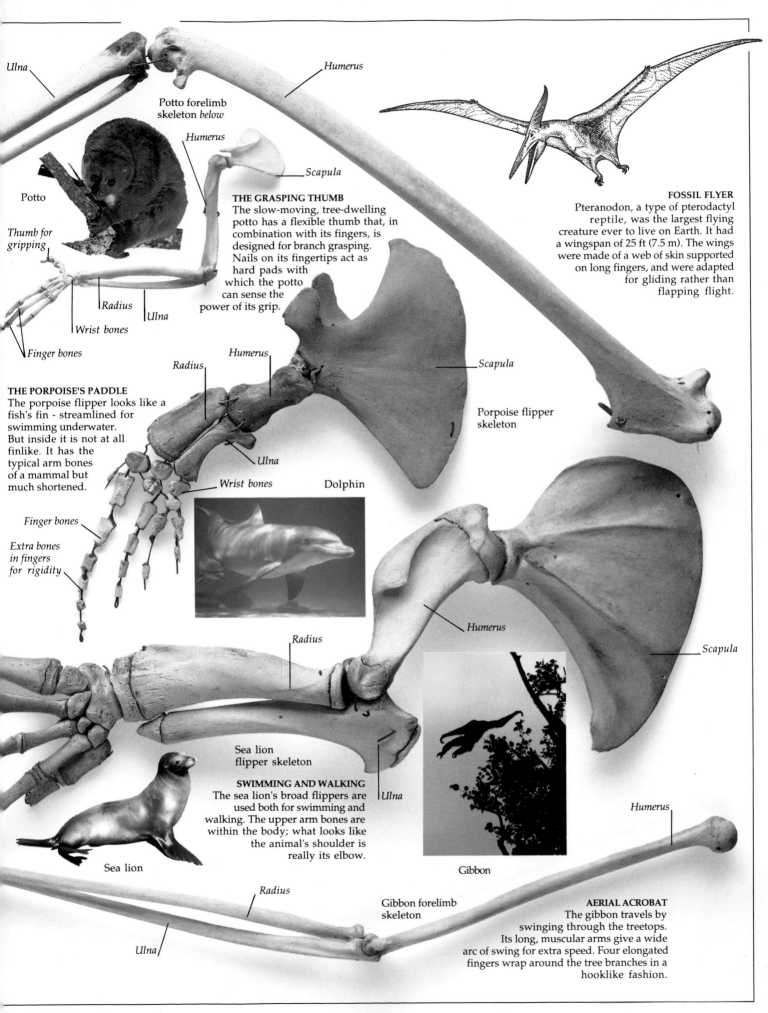

Ulna

Humerus

Potto forelimb
skeleton *below*

Humerus

Scapula

Potto

THE GRASPING THUMB
The slow-moving, tree-dwelling
potto has a flexible thumb that, in
combination with its fingers, is
designed for branch grasping.
Nails on its fingertips act as
hard pads with
which the potto
can sense the
power of its grip.

*Thumb for
gripping*

Radius

Ulna

Wrist bones

Finger bones

FOSSIL FLYER
Pteranodon, a type of pterodactyl
reptile, was the largest flying
creature ever to live on Earth. It had
a wingspan of 25 ft (7.5 m). The wings
were made of a web of skin supported
on long fingers, and were adapted
for gliding rather than
flapping flight.

Radius

Humerus

Scapula

Porpoise flipper
skeleton

THE PORPOISE'S PADDLE
The porpoise flipper looks like a
fish's fin - streamlined for
swimming underwater.
But inside it is not at all
finlike. It has the
typical arm bones
of a mammal but
much shortened.

Ulna

Wrist bones

Dolphin

Finger bones

*Extra bones
in fingers
for rigidity*

Radius

Humerus

Scapula

Radius

Sea lion
flipper skeleton

SWIMMING AND WALKING
The sea lion's broad flippers are
used both for swimming and
walking. The upper arm bones are
within the body; what looks like
the animal's shoulder is
really its elbow.

Ulna

Humerus

Sea lion

Gibbon

Radius

Gibbon forelimb
skeleton

Ulna

AERIAL ACROBAT
The gibbon travels by
swinging through the treetops.
Its long, muscular arms give a wide
arc of swing for extra speed. Four elongated
fingers wrap around the tree branches in a
hooklike fashion.

51

Animal shoulder blades

FROM THE OUTSIDE, the four limbs of a four-legged animal look much the same. But inside, the skeleton reveals many differences. The back legs are designed mainly for moving the whole body forward when walking, running, or jumping (p. 56). The front legs, on the other hand, do various jobs. They cushion the body when landing after a leap; they may move and hold food or objects; and they can strike at prey or enemies. So they need to be more flexible. The key to their wider range of movement is the shoulder blade, or scapula. This triangle of bone connects to the body chiefly by muscles that run to the backbone and ribs, and which can tilt the scapula at many angles. And it links to the forelimb by a ball-and-socket joint, giving even greater flexibility.

Red fox

Red fox shoulder blade

ON THE TROT
The fox's broad shoulder blade has a large surface area for muscle anchorage, indicating that it moves for much of the time on all fours. Foxes may also dig for food with their front legs.

Collared peccary shoulder blade

STIFF-LEGGED PIG
The long, narrow shoulder blade of the collared peccary, a type of pig, is swung forward and back by the muscles connecting it to the body. The legs are relatively short and thin, resulting in a rather stiff-legged walk.

Beaver holding twig it is gnawing

DAM BUILDER
The beaver's smallish shoulder blade shows that its short front limbs are not weight carriers. They are manipulators for holding food and prodding twigs and mud into dams.

Pig skeleton

Wallaby shoulder blade

CROUCHING TO DRINK
A Siberian tiger lowers itself over a pool to drink. Its spine is lowered between its front legs, and the shoulder blades show clearly on each side of the body.

Beaver shoulder blade

TWO-LEGGED HOPPING
The forelimbs of a kangaroo or wallaby take no part in its fast hopping movements. They are used to fight and play, to pick up food, and to lean on when grazing.

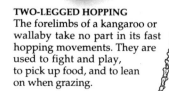

Kangaroo skeleton

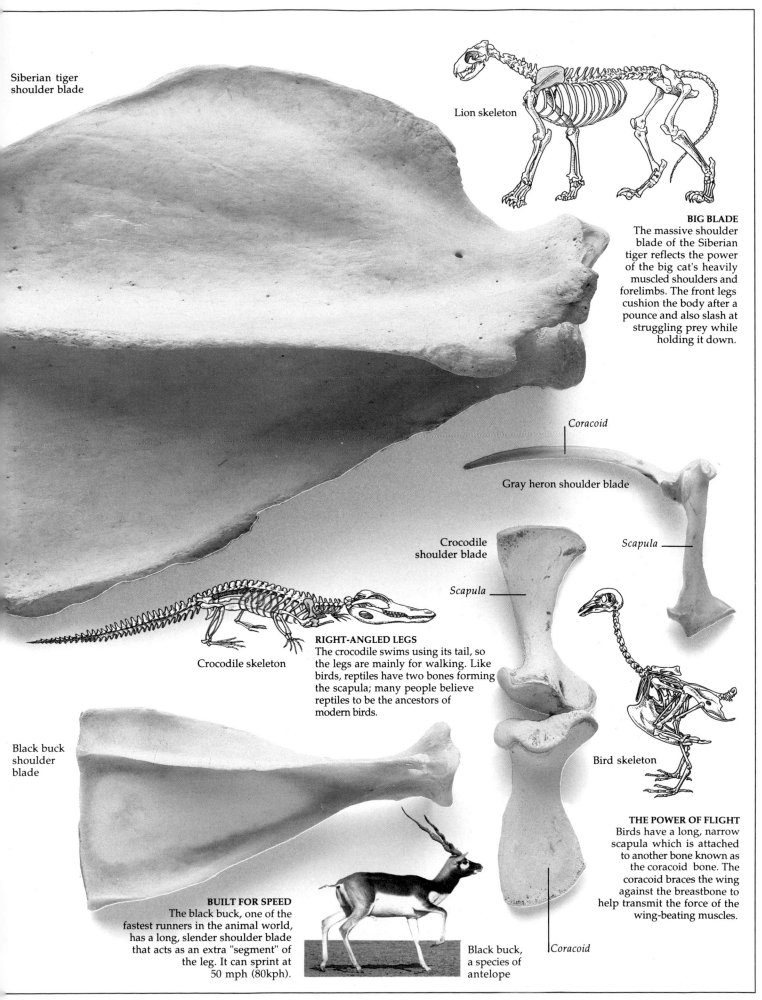

Siberian tiger
shoulder blade

Lion skeleton

BIG BLADE
The massive shoulder
blade of the Siberian
tiger reflects the power
of the big cat's heavily
muscled shoulders and
forelimbs. The front legs
cushion the body after a
pounce and also slash at
struggling prey while
holding it down.

Coracoid

Gray heron shoulder blade

Crocodile
shoulder blade

Scapula

Scapula

Crocodile skeleton

RIGHT-ANGLED LEGS
The crocodile swims using its tail, so
the legs are mainly for walking. Like
birds, reptiles have two bones forming
the scapula; many people believe
reptiles to be the ancestors of
modern birds.

Bird skeleton

Black buck
shoulder
blade

THE POWER OF FLIGHT
Birds have a long, narrow
scapula which is attached
to another bone known as
the coracoid bone. The
coracoid braces the wing
against the breastbone to
help transmit the force of the
wing-beating muscles.

BUILT FOR SPEED
The black buck, one of the
fastest runners in the animal world,
has a long, slender shoulder blade
that acts as an extra "segment" of
the leg. It can sprint at
50 mph (80kph).

Black buck,
a species of
antelope

Coracoid

The human leg and foot

Thigh bone (femur)

Head of thigh bone

WE ARE SO used to standing and watching the world go by that we are not usually aware of what an amazing balancing feat this is. Other animals may be able to stand on their back limbs temporarily, but they usually topple over after a few seconds. We can maintain a fully upright, two-legged posture for hours, leaving our arms and hands free for other tasks. Compared to the arm (p. 48), the bones of the human leg are thick and strong, to carry the body's weight. We do not walk on our toes, like many creatures (p. 56). Our feet are broad and also long, for good stability, and our toes are much smaller than in most other animals. Small muscle adjustments take place continuously in the neck, arms, back, and legs, keeping our weight over our feet. Walking requires the coordination and contraction of dozens of muscles. It has been called "controlled falling": the body tilts forwards, so that it begins to tip over, only to be saved from falling by moving a foot forward.

THE HEAD OF THE LEG
The thigh bone is the largest single bone in the body. At its top end, or "head", it is reinforced by ridges that anchor powerful leg-moving muscles.

LONG, YET STRONG
In accordance with good engineering design, the shaft of the thigh bone is long and tubelike. It is subjected to fewer stresses and strains along its length than at the ends.

SWINGING ARMS
As you walk, the arm on one side swings forward as the leg on that side swings back. The two movements partly cancel each other out, keeping the body's weight mostly in the center.

The muscles and joints of the leg

The muscles at the hip, thigh, and calf move the limbs at the joints. Those at the hip swing the leg forward and backward at the hip joint, as when walking. The muscles at the back of the thigh bend the knee at its hinge joint. Those in the calf straighten the foot at the ankle joint.

THE HIP
This ball-and-socket joint combines great strength with some mobility. The ball of the thigh bone is at an angle to the shaft so as to come more directly under the middle of the body.

THE KNEE
This joint works like a hinge, its main movements being forward and backward. It cannot cope with too much twisting, when it may become damaged.

MUSCLES FOR MOVING THE LEG
This rear view of the legs shows all the muscles important in movement.

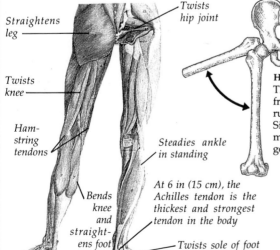

Straightens leg

Twists knee

Ham-string tendons

Bends knee and straightens foot

Twists hip joint

Steadies ankle in standing

At 6 in (15 cm), the Achilles tendon is the thickest and strongest tendon in the body

Twists sole of foot inwards

HIP LIMITS
The hip moves easily from front to back for running and walking. Side-to-side movement is limited but good for suddenly changing direction.

THE ANKLE
Seven bones make up the ankle, a composite joint. Each bone moves a little in relation to its neighbors, giving great overall strength with limited flexibility.

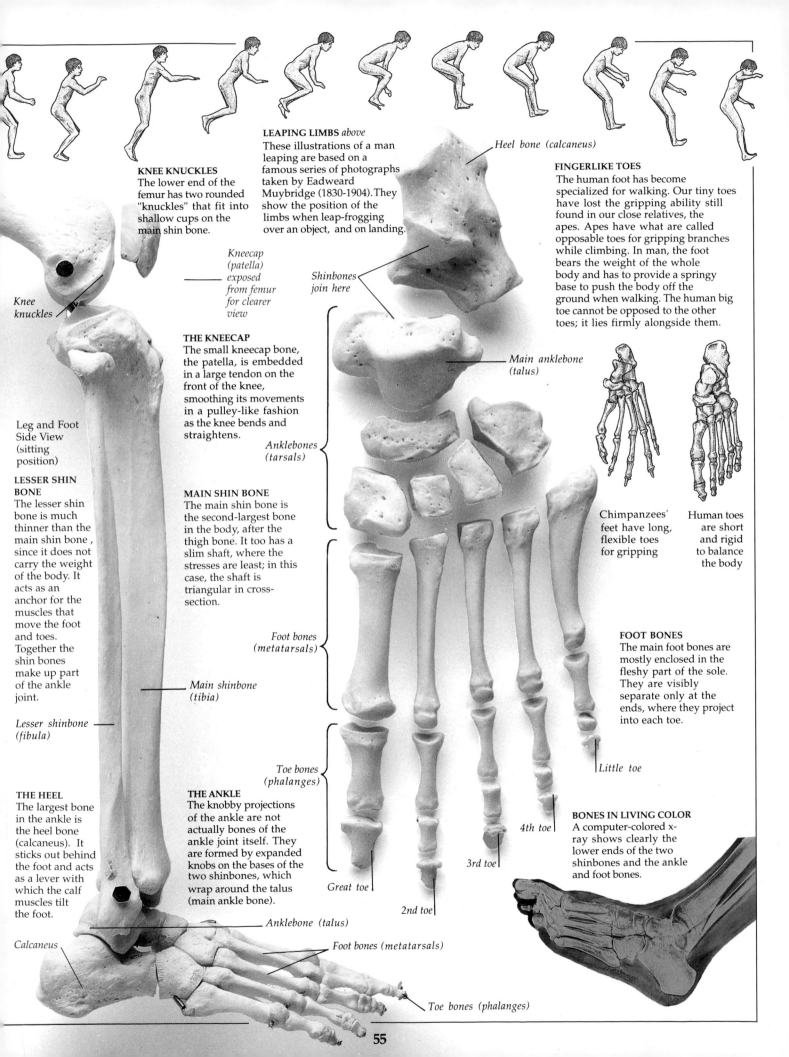

KNEE KNUCKLES
The lower end of the femur has two rounded "knuckles" that fit into shallow cups on the main shin bone.

LEAPING LIMBS *above*
These illustrations of a man leaping are based on a famous series of photographs taken by Eadweard Muybridge (1830-1904). They show the position of the limbs when leap-frogging over an object, and on landing.

Kneecap (patella) exposed from femur for clearer view

Heel bone (calcaneus)

FINGERLIKE TOES
The human foot has become specialized for walking. Our tiny toes have lost the gripping ability still found in our close relatives, the apes. Apes have what are called opposable toes for gripping branches while climbing. In man, the foot bears the weight of the whole body and has to provide a springy base to push the body off the ground when walking. The human big toe cannot be opposed to the other toes; it lies firmly alongside them.

Knee knuckles

Shinbones join here

THE KNEECAP
The small kneecap bone, the patella, is embedded in a large tendon on the front of the knee, smoothing its movements in a pulley-like fashion as the knee bends and straightens.

Main anklebone (talus)

Anklebones (tarsals)

Chimpanzees' feet have long, flexible toes for gripping

Human toes are short and rigid to balance the body

Leg and Foot Side View (sitting position)

LESSER SHIN BONE
The lesser shin bone is much thinner than the main shin bone, since it does not carry the weight of the body. It acts as an anchor for the muscles that move the foot and toes. Together the shin bones make up part of the ankle joint.

MAIN SHIN BONE
The main shin bone is the second-largest bone in the body, after the thigh bone. It too has a slim shaft, where the stresses are least; in this case, the shaft is triangular in cross-section.

Foot bones (metatarsals)

FOOT BONES
The main foot bones are mostly enclosed in the fleshy part of the sole. They are visibly separate only at the ends, where they project into each toe.

Little toe

Main shinbone (tibia)

Lesser shinbone (fibula)

Toe bones (phalanges)

4th toe

BONES IN LIVING COLOR
A computer-colored x-ray shows clearly the lower ends of the two shinbones and the ankle and foot bones.

THE HEEL
The largest bone in the ankle is the heel bone (calcaneus). It sticks out behind the foot and acts as a lever with which the calf muscles tilt the foot.

THE ANKLE
The knobby projections of the ankle are not actually bones of the ankle joint itself. They are formed by expanded knobs on the bases of the two shinbones, which wrap around the talus (main ankle bone).

Great toe

3rd toe

2nd toe

Calcaneus

Anklebone (talus)

Foot bones (metatarsals)

Toe bones (phalanges)

Animal legs

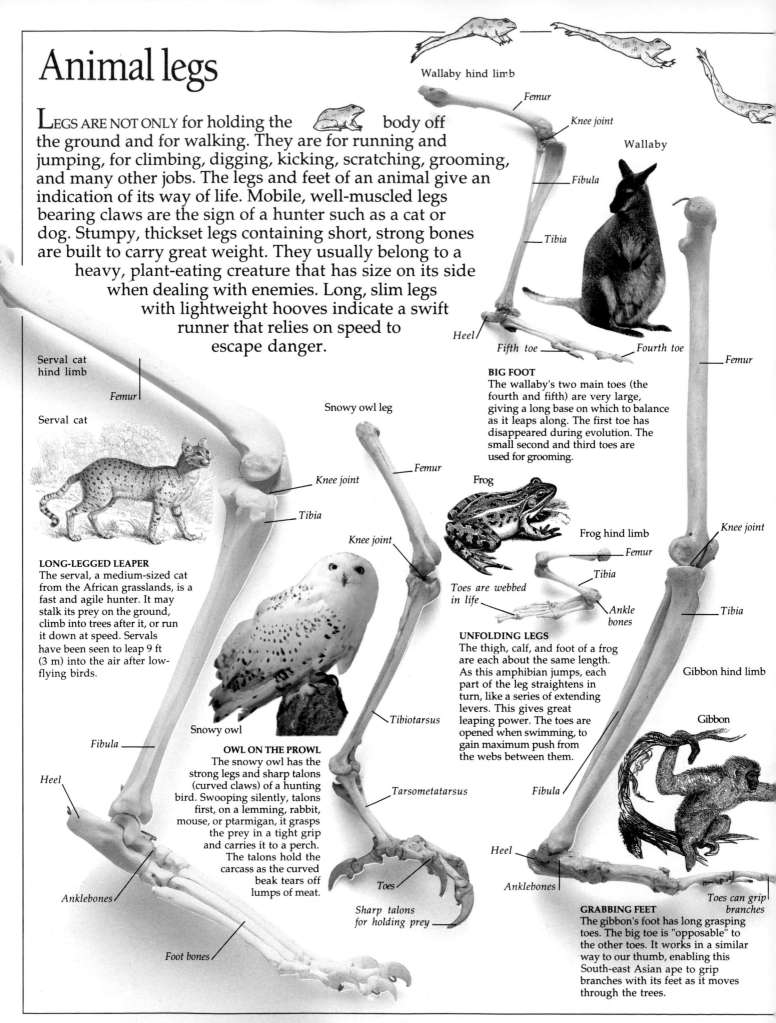

LEGS ARE NOT ONLY for holding the body off the ground and for walking. They are for running and jumping, for climbing, digging, kicking, scratching, grooming, and many other jobs. The legs and feet of an animal give an indication of its way of life. Mobile, well-muscled legs bearing claws are the sign of a hunter such as a cat or dog. Stumpy, thickset legs containing short, strong bones are built to carry great weight. They usually belong to a heavy, plant-eating creature that has size on its side when dealing with enemies. Long, slim legs with lightweight hooves indicate a swift runner that relies on speed to escape danger.

Wallaby hind limb

Femur

Knee joint

Wallaby

Fibula

Tibia

Heel

Fifth toe

Fourth toe

Femur

BIG FOOT
The wallaby's two main toes (the fourth and fifth) are very large, giving a long base on which to balance as it leaps along. The first toe has disappeared during evolution. The small second and third toes are used for grooming.

Serval cat hind limb

Femur

Serval cat

Snowy owl leg

Femur

Knee joint

Tibia

Frog

Frog hind limb

Femur

Tibia

Knee joint

Knee joint

Tibia

Toes are webbed in life

Ankle bones

LONG-LEGGED LEAPER
The serval, a medium-sized cat from the African grasslands, is a fast and agile hunter. It may stalk its prey on the ground, climb into trees after it, or run it down at speed. Servals have been seen to leap 9 ft (3 m) into the air after low-flying birds.

UNFOLDING LEGS
The thigh, calf, and foot of a frog are each about the same length. As this amphibian jumps, each part of the leg straightens in turn, like a series of extending levers. This gives great leaping power. The toes are opened when swimming, to gain maximum push from the webs between them.

Gibbon hind limb

Fibula

Snowy owl

Tibiotarsus

Gibbon

Heel

OWL ON THE PROWL
The snowy owl has the strong legs and sharp talons (curved claws) of a hunting bird. Swooping silently, talons first, on a lemming, rabbit, mouse, or ptarmigan, it grasps the prey in a tight grip and carries it to a perch. The talons hold the carcass as the curved beak tears off lumps of meat.

Tarsometatarsus

Fibula

Heel

Anklebones

Anklebones

Toes

Toes can grip branches

Foot bones

Sharp talons for holding prey

GRABBING FEET
The gibbon's foot has long grasping toes. The big toe is "opposable" to the other toes. It works in a similar way to our thumb, enabling this South-east Asian ape to grip branches with its feet as it moves through the trees.

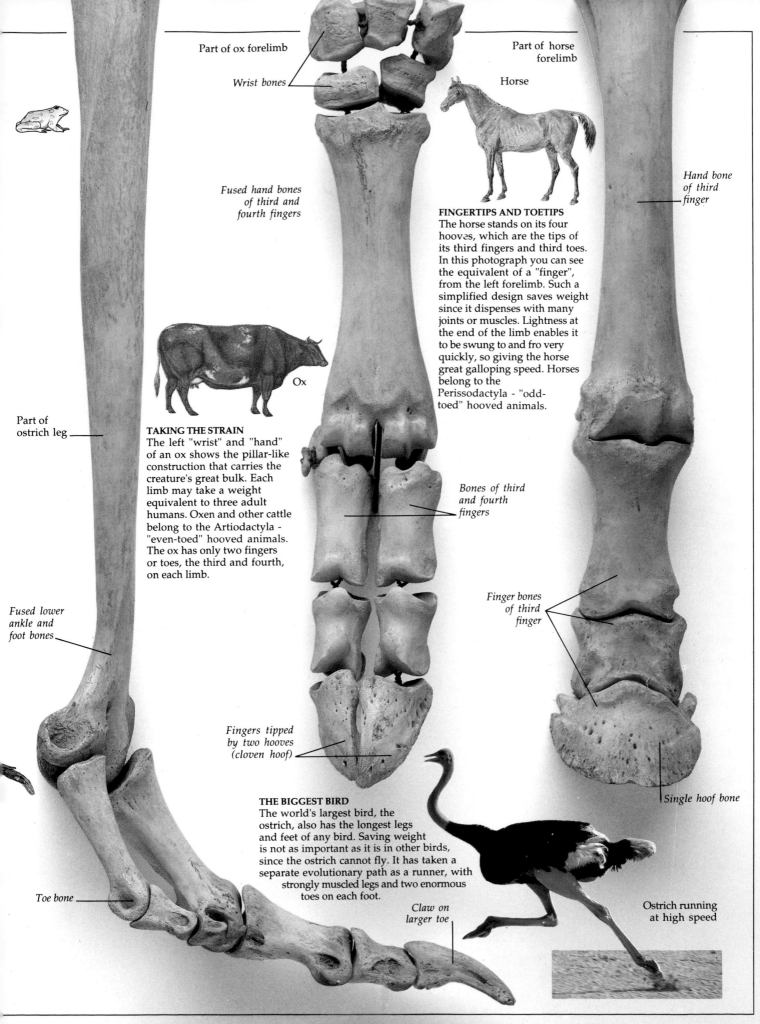

Part of ox forelimb

Wrist bones

Part of horse forelimb

Horse

Fused hand bones of third and fourth fingers

Hand bone of third finger

FINGERTIPS AND TOETIPS
The horse stands on its four hooves, which are the tips of its third fingers and third toes. In this photograph you can see the equivalent of a "finger", from the left forelimb. Such a simplified design saves weight since it dispenses with many joints or muscles. Lightness at the end of the limb enables it to be swung to and fro very quickly, so giving the horse great galloping speed. Horses belong to the Perissodactyla - "odd-toed" hooved animals.

Ox

TAKING THE STRAIN
The left "wrist" and "hand" of an ox shows the pillar-like construction that carries the creature's great bulk. Each limb may take a weight equivalent to three adult humans. Oxen and other cattle belong to the Artiodactyla - "even-toed" hooved animals. The ox has only two fingers or toes, the third and fourth, on each limb.

Part of ostrich leg

Bones of third and fourth fingers

Finger bones of third finger

Fused lower ankle and foot bones

Fingers tipped by two hooves (cloven hoof)

Single hoof bone

THE BIGGEST BIRD
The world's largest bird, the ostrich, also has the longest legs and feet of any bird. Saving weight is not as important as it is in other birds, since the ostrich cannot fly. It has taken a separate evolutionary path as a runner, with strongly muscled legs and two enormous toes on each foot.

Toe bone

Claw on larger toe

Ostrich running at high speed

The largest and smallest bones

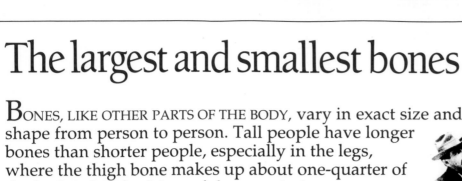
Giant Hugo

BONES, LIKE OTHER PARTS OF THE BODY, vary in exact size and shape from person to person. Tall people have longer bones than shorter people, especially in the legs, where the thigh bone makes up about one-quarter of the body's height. Most of these variations in bone length are slight, however, with the average man being taller than the average woman. Occasionally a disease or inherited condition affects development of bones as the baby grows in the womb. Or bone growth during childhood, which is controlled mainly by hormones, may be affected by disease, illness, or a poor diet. The result is an unusually tall or small person.

Reconstructed fossil skeleton of Iguanodon

VERY TALL
Gigantism is caused by a hormone condition that makes the bones grow very fast. Authentic records give the tallest man ever as American Robert Wadlow at 8 ft 11 in (2.7 m). Above is another famous American, Giant Hugo.

VERY SMALL
The smallest humans measure about 2 ft to 2 ft 6 in (60 cm to 75 cm). One of the best-known midgets, shown here with his midget wife, was Charles Stratton ("General Tom Thumb") who was 3 ft 4 in (1.02 m) short.

"Tom Thumb" at his wedding

ANIMAL GIANTS
Dinosaurs, the largest land animals ever, had gigantic bones. The thigh bone of this Iguanodon (p. 12) was 4 ft 3 in (1.3 m) long. Some dinosaur arm bones were nearly 9 ft (3 m) long!

The size of the thighs

This array of 10 thigh bones (femurs) shows the enormous size differences within the mammal group. In general, fast-moving animals have long, slender leg bones in relation to their body size. The seal's femurs are a special case: they are within the body, and this animal swims using its back flippers, which contain its shin and feet bones.

SHEEP *left*
Body length - 4 ft 8 in (1.4 m)
Femur length - 7 in (18 cm)

RABBIT
Body length - 12 in (30 cm)
Femur length - 3 in (8 cm)

HEDGEHOG
Body length - 8 in (20 cm)
Femur length - 1.6 in (4 cm)

SEAL
Body length - 5 ft (1.6 m)
Femur length - 4.5 in (11 cm)

DOG (BASSET HOUND)
Body length - 2 ft 4 in (70 cm)
Femur length - 4.5 in (11 cm)

CAT *left*
Body length - 1 ft 8 in (50 cm)
Femur length - 5 in (12 cm)

ROE DEER *right*
Body length - 3 ft (1 m)
Femur length - 7 in (18 cm)

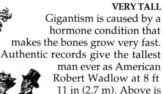

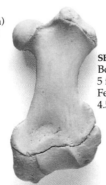

The smallest bones in the body

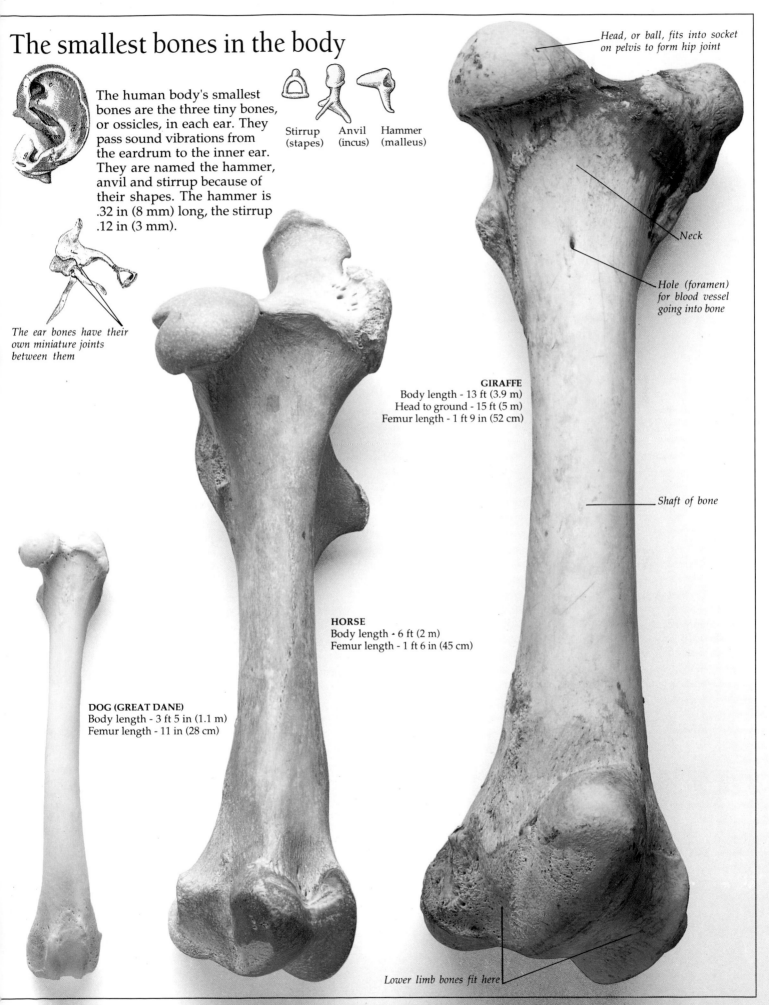

The human body's smallest bones are the three tiny bones, or ossicles, in each ear. They pass sound vibrations from the eardrum to the inner ear. They are named the hammer, anvil and stirrup because of their shapes. The hammer is .32 in (8 mm) long, the stirrup .12 in (3 mm).

Stirrup (stapes) Anvil (incus) Hammer (malleus)

The ear bones have their own miniature joints between them

Head, or ball, fits into socket on pelvis to form hip joint

Neck

Hole (foramen) for blood vessel going into bone

GIRAFFE
Body length - 13 ft (3.9 m)
Head to ground - 15 ft (5 m)
Femur length - 1 ft 9 in (52 cm)

Shaft of bone

HORSE
Body length - 6 ft (2 m)
Femur length - 1 ft 6 in (45 cm)

DOG (GREAT DANE)
Body length - 3 ft 5 in (1.1 m)
Femur length - 11 in (28 cm)

Lower limb bones fit here

Structure and repair of bones

LIVING BONES ARE NOT PALE, dry, and brittle, as they are in a museum case. Bone in the body is a busy living tissue. It is one-third water; it has blood vessels going in and out of it, supplying oxygen and nutrients and taking away wastes; certain bones contain marrow which produces blood cells; and bones have nerves that can feel pressure and pain. Bone is also a mineral store, containing calcium and other chemicals which give it hardness and rigidity. However, bone will give up its minerals in times of shortage, when other parts of the body (such as nerves) need them more. Bone tissue is made and maintained by several types of cells. Osteoblasts make new bone by hardening the protein collagen with minerals. Osteocytes maintain bone, passing nutrients and wastes back and forth between the blood and bone tissues. Osteoclasts destroy bone, releasing the minerals into the blood. All through life, bone is continually being reconstructed and reshaped as a result of the stresses, bends, and breaks it endures.

ISOTOPE SCAN
Radioactive isotopes concentrate in bone, and a scan shows their distribution in the skeleton.

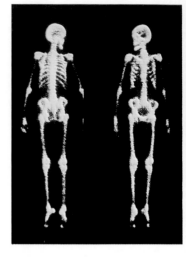

LIVING BONE
There are many ways of looking at living bones besides x-rays. By means of a pulsing crystal, this "scintigram" detects the concentrations of a radioactive isotope, which is injected into the body and taken up by bone tissue.

Inside bone

Bones are living examples of the engineer's art of design. Most bones have an outer "shell" of hard, solid, ivory-like compact bone. Tendons, ligaments, and other parts attach to this rigid shell by way of the living bone's "skin," the periosteum. Inside the compact bone is a looser, lighter network of spongy bone that contains the marrow.

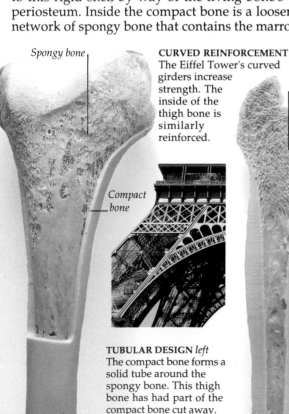

Spongy bone

Compact bone

CURVED REINFORCEMENT
The Eiffel Tower's curved girders increase strength. The inside of the thigh bone is similarly reinforced.

TUBULAR DESIGN *left*
The compact bone forms a solid tube around the spongy bone. This thigh bone has had part of the compact bone cut away.

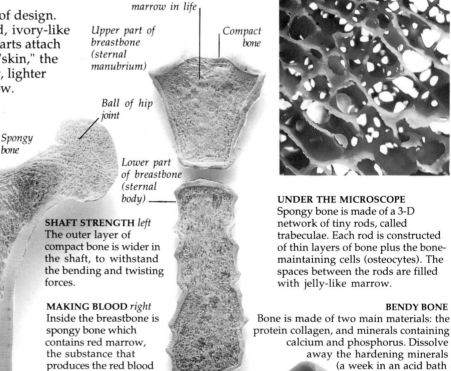

Spongy bone

Spongy bone contains red bone marrow in life

Upper part of breastbone (sternal manubrium)

Compact bone

Ball of hip joint

Lower part of breastbone (sternal body)

SHAFT STRENGTH *left*
The outer layer of compact bone is wider in the shaft, to withstand the bending and twisting forces.

MAKING BLOOD *right*
Inside the breastbone is spongy bone which contains red marrow, the substance that produces the red blood cells.

Wide layer of compact bone for strength

UNDER THE MICROSCOPE
Spongy bone is made of a 3-D network of tiny rods, called trabeculae. Each rod is constructed of thin layers of bone plus the bone-maintaining cells (osteocytes). The spaces between the rods are filled with jelly-like marrow.

BENDY BONE
Bone is made of two main materials: the protein collagen, and minerals containing calcium and phosphorus. Dissolve away the hardening minerals (a week in an acid bath will do it) and the collagen is flexible enough to tie in a knot!

Breaks and mends

Since bone is an active living tissue, it can usually mend itself after a crack or break (fracture). The gap is bridged first by fiber-like material, to form a scar or callus. Then bone-making cells (osteoblasts) gradually move into the callus and harden it into true bone. This is usually a little lumpy around the edges, so bone-destroying cells (osteoclasts) sculpt the bumps to produce a smooth mend.

FROM BREAK TO MEND
Broken bones mend mainly in response to stresses. A dog broke its two forearm bones (below). The main weight-bearing bone mended well; the other, which carried hardly any weight, never really knitted together.

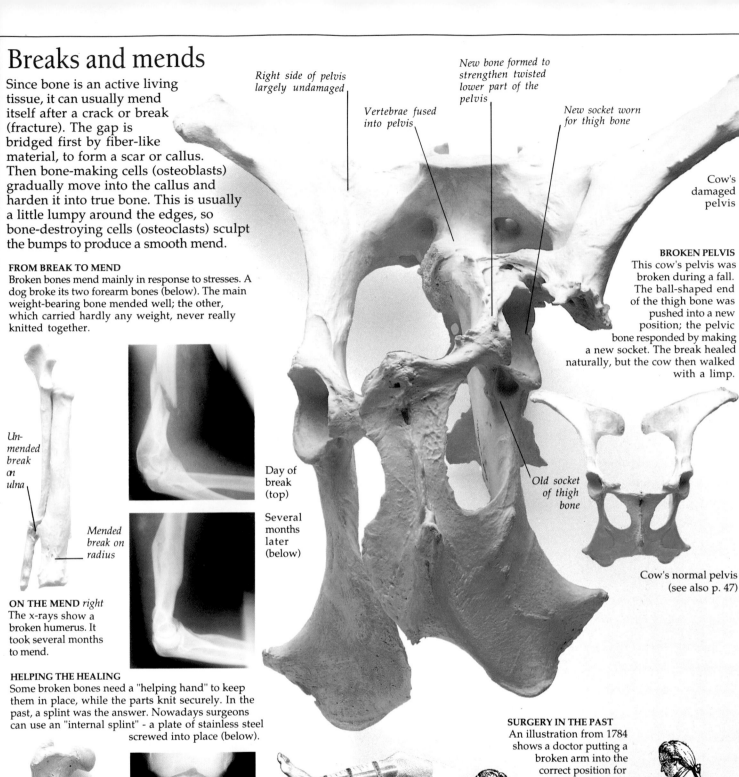

Right side of pelvis largely undamaged

Vertebrae fused into pelvis

New bone formed to strengthen twisted lower part of the pelvis

New socket worn for thigh bone

Cow's damaged pelvis

Un-mended break on ulna

Mended break on radius

Day of break (top)

Several months later (below)

Old socket of thigh bone

BROKEN PELVIS
This cow's pelvis was broken during a fall. The ball-shaped end of the thigh bone was pushed into a new position; the pelvic bone responded by making a new socket. The break healed naturally, but the cow then walked with a limp.

Cow's normal pelvis (see also p. 47)

ON THE MEND *right*
The x-rays show a broken humerus. It took several months to mend.

HELPING THE HEALING
Some broken bones need a "helping hand" to keep them in place, while the parts knit securely. In the past, a splint was the answer. Nowadays surgeons can use an "internal splint" - a plate of stainless steel screwed into place (below).

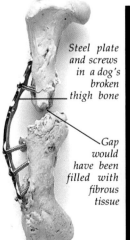

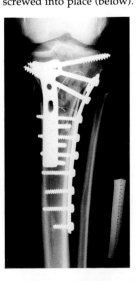

Steel plate and screws in a dog's broken thigh bone

Gap would have been filled with fibrous tissue

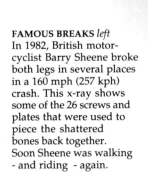

Splint for rigidity while the bone heals

SURGERY IN THE PAST
An illustration from 1784 shows a doctor putting a broken arm into the correct position for healing, using a plank splint.

FAMOUS BREAKS *left*
In 1982, British motor-cyclist Barry Sheene broke both legs in several places in a 160 mph (257 kph) crash. This x-ray shows some of the 26 screws and plates that were used to piece the shattered bones back together. Soon Sheene was walking - and riding - again.

Glossary of bone names

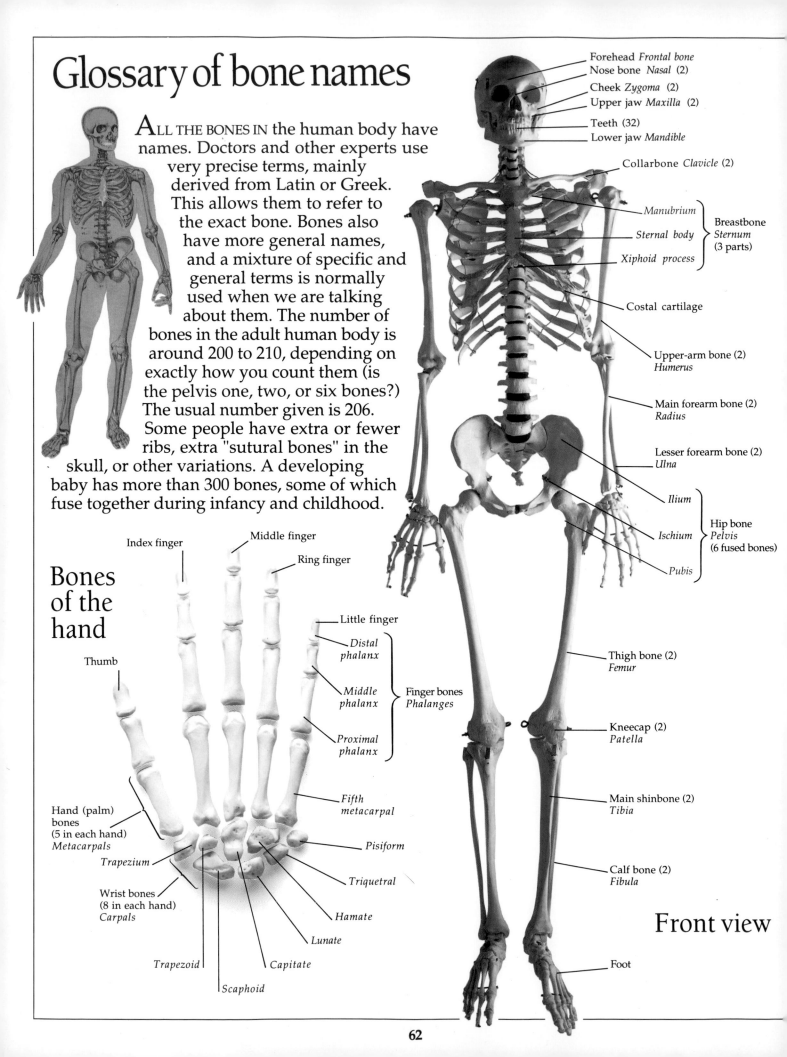

ALL THE BONES IN the human body have names. Doctors and other experts use very precise terms, mainly derived from Latin or Greek. This allows them to refer to the exact bone. Bones also have more general names, and a mixture of specific and general terms is normally used when we are talking about them. The number of bones in the adult human body is around 200 to 210, depending on exactly how you count them (is the pelvis one, two, or six bones?) The usual number given is 206. Some people have extra or fewer ribs, extra "sutural bones" in the skull, or other variations. A developing baby has more than 300 bones, some of which fuse together during infancy and childhood.

Forehead *Frontal bone*
Nose bone *Nasal* (2)
Cheek *Zygoma* (2)
Upper jaw *Maxilla* (2)
Teeth (32)
Lower jaw *Mandible*

Collarbone *Clavicle* (2)

Manubrium
Sternal body — Breastbone *Sternum* (3 parts)
Xiphoid process

Costal cartilage

Upper-arm bone (2) *Humerus*

Main forearm bone (2) *Radius*

Lesser forearm bone (2) *Ulna*

Ilium
Ischium — Hip bone *Pelvis* (6 fused bones)
Pubis

Thigh bone (2) *Femur*

Kneecap (2) *Patella*

Main shinbone (2) *Tibia*

Calf bone (2) *Fibula*

Front view

Foot

Bones of the hand

Index finger
Middle finger
Ring finger
Little finger

Distal phalanx
Middle phalanx — Finger bones *Phalanges*
Proximal phalanx

Thumb

Fifth metacarpal

Pisiform

Triquetral

Hamate

Lunate

Hand (palm) bones (5 in each hand) *Metacarpals*

Trapezium

Wrist bones (8 in each hand) *Carpals*

Trapezoid
Capitate
Scaphoid

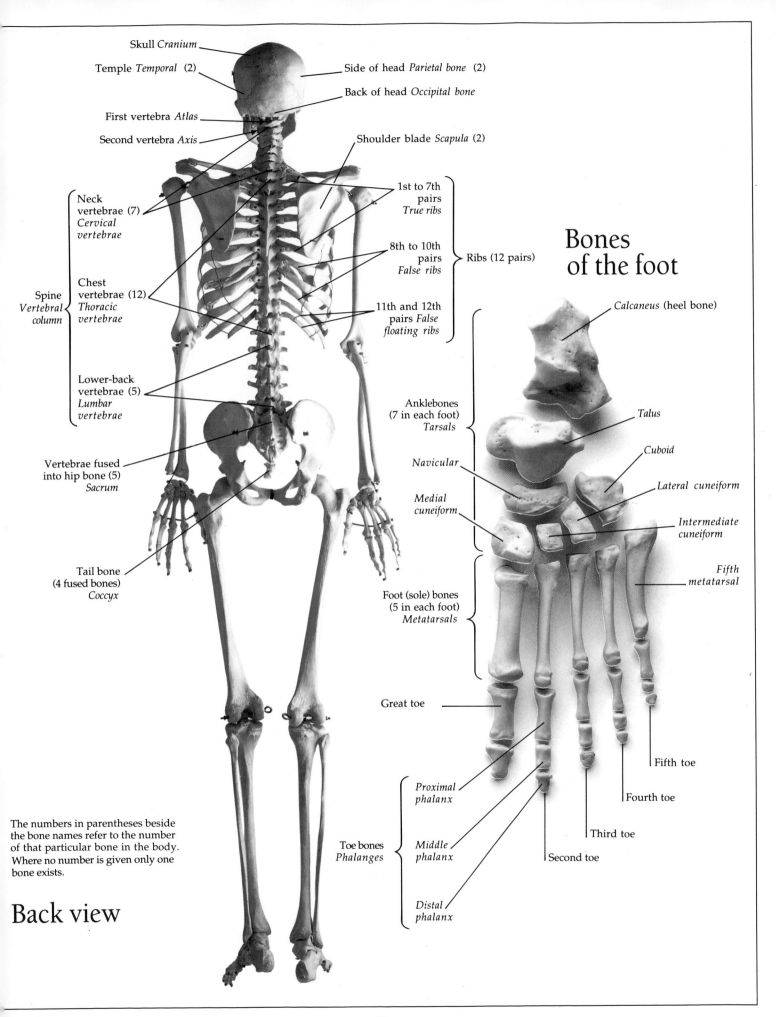

Skull *Cranium*

Temple *Temporal* (2)

Side of head *Parietal bone* (2)

Back of head *Occipital bone*

First vertebra *Atlas*

Second vertebra *Axis*

Shoulder blade *Scapula* (2)

Neck vertebrae (7) *Cervical vertebrae*

1st to 7th pairs *True ribs*

8th to 10th pairs *False ribs*

Ribs (12 pairs)

Spine *Vertebral column*

Chest vertebrae (12) *Thoracic vertebrae*

11th and 12th pairs *False floating ribs*

Lower-back vertebrae (5) *Lumbar vertebrae*

Vertebrae fused into hip bone (5) *Sacrum*

Tail bone (4 fused bones) *Coccyx*

Bones of the foot

Calcaneus (heel bone)

Talus

Cuboid

Lateral cuneiform

Intermediate cuneiform

Anklebones (7 in each foot) *Tarsals*

Navicular

Medial cuneiform

Fifth metatarsal

Foot (sole) bones (5 in each foot) *Metatarsals*

Great toe

Proximal phalanx

Fifth toe

Fourth toe

Third toe

Second toe

Toe bones *Phalanges*

Middle phalanx

Distal phalanx

The numbers in parentheses beside the bone names refer to the number of that particular bone in the body. Where no number is given only one bone exists.

Back view

Did you know?

Pound for pound, bone is five times stronger than steel.

Compact bone is the second hardest material in the body. The hardest is tooth enamel.

People who are "double jointed" do not actually have extra joints, they just have looser ligaments.

Some people have extra tiny bones, called sesamoid bones, that grow within their tendons. These bones most often form in the hands and feet.

If a lizard loses its tail, it can grow a new one. In fact, the bones in a lizard's tail have special break points designed to fracture easily if the lizard is caught. The twitching, severed tail then distracts the predator, allowing the rest of the lizard to escape.

Three stages in the regrowth of a lizard's tail

Sharks, rays, and skates do not have any bones at all— their skeletons are made up entirely of cartilage.

When a person has a badly fractured bone that will not heal, surgeons can sometimes take bone chips from the pelvis and place them in the break. The chips grow to fill the gaps and heal the bone.

The axolotl, a type of salamander, is able to grow new legs and a new tail after a predator attack. It can even grow back some of its feathery external gills.

Some owls have ears on different levels. Each ear picks up a sound at a slightly different time, allowing pinpoint accuracy of the sound's direction.

The American Indian Blackfeet and Dakota tribes used to paint the skulls of buffalo and decorate them with sage and grass as part of their ritual Sun Dance.

The base of a coral reef is made up of the calcium-rich skeletal remains of millions of tiny coral animals. The longest reef in the world is the Great Barrier Reef in Australia, which stretches for about 1,250 miles (2,010 km).

Contrary to popular belief, men and women have exactly the same number of ribs.

When a child grows, bones such as the thighbone (femur) do not grow evenly from all points along their length. Instead, they grow only from the ends.

In a fall, a baby is less likely to break a bone than an adult. This is partly because a baby is lighter than an adult, but mostly it is because a baby's bones are not yet fully formed. A baby's skeleton has a lot of soft, flexible cartilage that will slowly turn into hard bone as the child grows.

Both sharks and crocodiles are continually growing sharp new teeth. When they catch prey, they often break or lose teeth, but new ones soon grow to replace them. A shark may grow more than 20,000 teeth in its lifetime.

Horn, a core of bone surrounded by horn protein (keratin)

A buffalo skull specially painted to be placed at an altar in the Blackfeet Sun Dance.

More than half the bones in a human are in the wrists, hands, ankles, and feet.

Horn is made up of many compressed hair fibers, and hair is made from the structural protein keratin, which also forms nails and feathers.

Around one fifth of a person's total body weight comes from just the bones and teeth.

Most people have 12 pairs of ribs, however, five percent of the population is born with one or more extra ribs. Some people, on the other hand, have only 11 pairs of ribs.

Orca (killer whale) skeleton

Chevrons, V-shaped bones where muscles join the backbone

An orca, or killer whale, swims using its powerful tail. Although it has no back legs, many whales do have a few vestigial (small, unused) leg bones, indicating that their ancestors once walked on land.

In order to avoid weak and brittle bones in older age, it is important to do weight-bearing exercise, such as walking, and to eat a healthy diet that includes plenty of calcium when you are young. Calcium-rich foods include milk, yogurt, broccoli, spinach, hard cheese, tofu, canned sardines, and salmon.

A cuttlefish "bone," such as those used by pet birds to sharpen their beaks, is in fact the living cuttlefish's internal shell. In addition to providing structural support, the shell helps the animal move around. The cuttlefish fills the tiny air spaces within the shell with gas to make itself rise, and then replaces the gas with fluid to make itself sink.

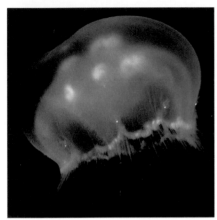

Jellyfish swim by expanding and contracting their bodies.

Some jellyfish can grow to 6 ft 6 in (2 m) long, and yet they have neither an external nor an internal skeleton—they get all the support they need from the surrounding seawater.

In the same way that humans lose their baby teeth as they grow up, young elephants lose their milk tusks when they are about one year old.

A single molar (grinding tooth) from an adult elephant weighs about 10 lb (4.5 kg). That's heavier than a brick.

By examining a skull, forensic scientists can work out what its owner may have looked like when alive. With use of either clay models or computer programs, they can build up the person's features based on the shapes of the bones. This method is used both to work out the identity of long-dead murder victims and to study people from ancient cultures.

Forensic scientists are now able to extract DNA, a chemical found in all body cells, from the skeleton of a murder victim. This can enable them to figure out the identity of a victim from just one small piece of bone or other tissue from any part of the body.

Fossil of *Sparnodus*, a fish that lived about 55 million years ago

The word "petrify" means to turn a once-living plant or animal into stone. Some fossils are formed when minerals dissolved in water flow into the gaps in buried bones, slowly strengthening the bone and turning it into solid, long-lasting rock.

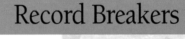

Record Breakers

TALLEST LIVING LAND ANIMAL
Giraffes have the tallest skeleton of any living land animal. They can reach 19.5 ft (6 m), as tall as three men.

LARGEST SKELETON
The blue whale has the largest skeleton of any living animal. It measures about 110 ft (33.5 m) in length.

LONGEST REPTILE SKELETON
The saltwater crocodile's skeleton can reach a length of 33 ft (10 m).

SMALLEST BIRD SKELETON
The tiny skeleton of the male bee hummingbird grows to only about 2.25 in (5.7 cm) in length. That's not much bigger than many moths.

LARGEST SPIDER SKELETON
The exoskeleton of the enormous goliath bird-eating spider from South America can reach a width of up to 11 in (28 cm) across the span of its legs.

LARGEST CRUSTACEAN
The exoskeleton of the Japanese spider crab can reach a width of up to 13 ft (4 m) across the span of its claws.

LARGEST FOSSIL BIRD
The wing bones of *Argentavis magnificens*, a prehistoric bird, spanned 25 ft (7.6 m).

LARGEST FOSSIL INSECT
The largest prehistoric insect on record is the 300-million-year-old dragonfly, *Meganeura monyi*. Its wings could span up to 29.5 in (75 cm).

Giraffe

A giraffe has only seven neck bones, the same number as a human.

Powerful jaws and strong teeth

Did you know? (continued)

Q Why does a hermit crab live inside a mollusk shell?

A Unlike most crabs, the hermit crab does not have a hard outer shell on its abdomen. This makes it vulnerable to attack, so it lives inside an old mollusk shell for protection. As it grows larger, it discards its cramped shell for a larger one.

Hermit crab in an artificial glass shell

Q If bones don't bend, how can exercise make my body more flexible?

A Bones that meet at a joint are held in place by ligaments. Careful exercise can slowly stretch these ligaments, enabling the joints to have a greater range of movement.

Q Why doesn't a snake break its rib cage when it swallows a large animal whole?

A A snake has no breastbone. Instead the ribs are joined by flexible muscles. Also, the joints in a snake's backbone are very loose, allowing the body to coil and bend in all directions.

Q Why do cats' "knees" bend backward?

A The bones on a cat that are equivalent to a human's knees are high up near the abdomen. The joints that look like knees are actually the equivalent of our ankles, which is why they bend the other way. Cats usually walk on just their toes, which enables them to run very swiftly.

Q Why is regular exercise good for your bones?

A Exercise tones your muscles, enabling them to hold the bones in their correct positions, preventing health problems such as backache and bad posture. Regular weight-bearing exercise, such as walking or running, also improves your bone mass: It helps increase the amount of calcium stored in your bones.

Q How does an insect move its hard exoskeleton?

A The hard plates that make up an insect's exoskeleton meet at flexible joints. Muscles attached to the exoskeleton across the insides of these joints contract to produce movement; four different muscles pull each limb forward, backward, upward, and downward.

Q Do worms have a skeleton?

A A worm does not have bones or cartilage, but it does have what is known as a hydrostatic skeleton. Its body is divided into separate segments, or cavities, that are filled with fluid. The fluid fills out the worm's body in a similar way that tap water can fill a balloon.

Q How do huge whales manage to find and eat krill and other minute sea creatures?

A A baleen whale, such as a right whale or a humpback whale, does not have teeth. Instead, it has rows of fringed plates that hang inside its mouth and filter food from the seawater. Like human hair and nails, the plates are made of the protein keratin, although they are sometimes inaccurately referred to as "whalebone."

Q Do whales have tusks?

A Most whales don't have tusks, but the male narwhal whale, which lives in remote parts of the Arctic and sub-Arctic, usually has one very long spiraling ivory tusk that can reach as long as 8 ft (2.4 m). Some people believe that narwhal tusks washed up on the seashore may have given rise to the unicorn myth.

A hoverfly

Q Why does the hoverfly have black-and-yellow stripes like a wasp?

A Some harmless insects, such as the hoverfly, protect themselves by mimicking the appearance of dangerous ones. The stingless hoverfly's exoskeleton resembles that of a wasp so that predators, such as birds, will leave it alone.

Q How do x-ray machines see through skin to the bones?

A X-ray machines fire out a beam of invisible rays. These rays can travel straight through skin and other soft body tissue, but not bone. When a piece of photographic film is placed behind the body, the x-rays go through the soft tissue and expose the film, turning it a darker color. The denser bones act like a stencil, preventing the rays from reaching the film directly behind them. They leave behind a white unexposed image of the bones' shapes.

Spiraling tusk

Male narwhal whale

Q Do our bones have any other roles apart from supporting the body?

A Yes, both our red and white blood cells are made inside the bones. The red blood cells carry oxygen around the body, and the white ones destroy disease-causing organisms such as bacteria and viruses.

Q How does a spider molt its exoskeleton?

A Before each molt, a spider partially digests and absorbs the old exoskeleton, preserving minerals and starting to break it down. Lubricating fluid between the old and new cuticle then helps the spider shed the old skin, revealing the new one. The new skeleton stays soft for a short time, allowing the spider to grow.

Tarantula molt

Q Why do flatfish, such as flounder, have both their eyes on the same side of their head?

A The skeletons of flatfish have adapted to allow these animals to live on the seabed. Their flat shape prevents them from being seen by predators and prey alike. Both their eyes are on the upward-facing side of the body, and they also have a special cavity in their flat skeleton to allow for the heart and other organs.

Q Do animals with beaks have teeth?

A Birds do not have teeth as the weight of teeth would make their skeleton too heavy for flight. Some beaked marine animals, however, do have teeth. The common dolphin, for example, has about 50 pairs of teeth in its upper and lower jaws. It uses them to grip food, which it swallows whole.

Q Why are bones breakable?

A Because our bones are hollow, they break more easily than they would if they were solid all the way through. However, if our bones were solid, our skeleton would be too heavy for us to carry or move around.

Q Why do some animals have eyes that face forward, while other have eyes that point in opposite directions?

A Predatory animals (animals that hunt) often have two forward-facing eyes. This gives them a wide field of binocular vision, which is three-dimensional and enables them to pinpoint prey very accurately. Animals that are hunted, on the other hand, often have eyes that point in opposite directions. This enables them to look for danger all around and above themselves without needing to turn their heads.

Q Why are the exoskeletons of beetles and other insects so colorful?

A Often the only visible part of animals such as beetles and other insects is their exoskeleton. Some poisonous beetles are brightly colored to warm potential prey not to eat them. Other beetles are colored green or brown to blend in with surrounding plant matter and avoid being seen by predators.

Q What is the difference between tusks and teeth?

A There is no real difference: Tusks are teeth that project beyond the jaw. A walrus's tusks are elongated canine teeth, and an elephant's tusks are elongated incisors.

Q Is the part of a horse's hoof that we can see really its toe bone?

A No, the hoof surrounds and protects the fragile toe or finger bones. When the horse is alive, a pad of fat lies between the bones and the hoof to act as a shock absorber.

A horse's toe bones sit inside the hoof.

Sleeping parakeet

Q Why don't birds fall off their perches when they get tired or sleep?

A When a bird perches on a branch, it bends its legs and rests its weight on the bones in its feet. This pulls the leg tendons tight, clamping the toes around the branch. To release its grip, the bird must contract its toe muscles.

Male moose with antlers

Q What is the difference between horns and antlers?

A True horns are simple, unbranched structures that are never shed. They are composed of a bony core surrounded by a softer outer layer of horn protein (keratin). Horns are found on cattle, sheep, goats, and antelopes. Antlers, on the other hand, are branched structures that are shed and regrown. They are composed entirely of bone, and in life, they are covered with a furry, velvetlike skin. They are found on elk, including moose, and deer.

Find out more

If you are interested in finding out more about skeletons, there are plenty of different ways you can do so. One of the most interesting options is to visit a museum. Most natural history museums are packed with skeletons of everything from spiders to dinosaurs. Many science museums have interactive exhibits that allow you to hold and investigate model bones, so you can see for yourself how they fit together and move. Some historical museums display the skeletons of ancient peoples, along with other artifacts such as clothing, household implements, and tools.

Other ways you can find out more about skeletons include searching the Internet and investigating the books, CD-ROMs, and videos at your local library. You might even want to find out about possible careers that involve working with bones, such as paleontology or physical therapy.

A PALEONTOLOGIST AT WORK
A paleontologist is a scientist who studies the bones of fossils, such as dinosaurs. Many paleontologists work in museums, where admission fees and grants help pay for their research. When museum visitors see a dinosaur on display, they are seeing the final results of years of planning and hard work.

A *T. rex* skeleton at the American Museum of Natural History in New York

MUSEUM
This museum technician is using a pair of callipers to measure the jaw of a bottle-nosed dolphin. The information she collects may be used to help construct models of the dolphin for display in the museum. Once her work is completed, the bones themselves may be put on display in the museum for visitors to view.

A physical therapist using a skeleton to help discuss a patient's condition

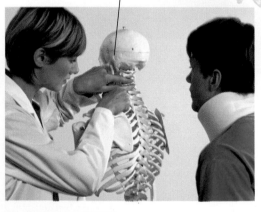

BONES AND MEDICINE
The first time many of us become aware of our bones is when we have a health problem. Physical therapists, doctors, and many other health-care professionals have studied the human skeleton in detail and can often answer any questions we have.

USEFUL WEB SITES

- A health-based site with information about the human skeleton:
  www.innerbody.com/htm/body.html

- A site that allows visitors to view, compare, and read about the bones of a human, a gorilla, and a baboon:
  www.eskeletons.org

- An interesting Web site featuring the largest *T. rex* ever found:
  www.fmnh.org/sue

- This Web site features short educational movies about bones:
  www.brainpop.com/health/skeletal

- A site about human and animal skeletons for young children:
  www.enchantedlearning.com/themes/skeleton.shtml

- An educational site with a fun quiz for older children:
  www.kidport.com/grade5/science/bodybones.htm

STUDYING BONES
Children often learn about bones in science class. Older children and adults can learn more about them by choosing to study biology. Medical students learn even more in anatomy class, in which they study the structure of the body in detail.

MODEL MAKING
A fun, hands-on way to really understand how bones fit together is to construct a model skeleton. Science supply shops, craft shops, and toy stores often sell kits of human, dinosaur, or other skeletons. They come in varying complexities to suit all ages.

Model skeleton constructed out of paper

Places to Visit

THE AMERICAN MUSEUM OF NATURAL HISTORY, NEW YORK, NY
Home to the world's largest collection of vertebrate fossils, this museum has two exceptional dinosaur halls. There is also a hall of mammals that includes the fossils of seals, bears, horses, whales, and more—and extinct animals such as mammoths, mastodons, saber-toothed cats, and the giant ground sloths that once roamed North America.

THE NATIONAL MUSEUM OF NATURAL HISTORY, SMITHSONIAN INSTITUTION, WASHINGTON, D.C.
The museum houses a large collection of dinosaur bones and information on some of the myths surrounding dinosaur extinction.

THE FIELD MUSEUM, CHICAGO, IL
See Sue, the largest, most complete, and best preserved skeleton fossil of a *T. rex* yet discovered. Visitors can come eye-to-eye with Sue's separately displayed skull and touch casts of selected bones to "diagnose" some of her wounds.

THE NATURAL HISTORY MUSEUM OF LOS ANGELES COUNTY, CA
The skeleton of a 14.5-foot-long Megamouth, the world's rarest shark, makes its home here. Also on view are dinosaurs including Mamenchisaurus, the largest-necked dinosaur ever discovered.

Lion skull

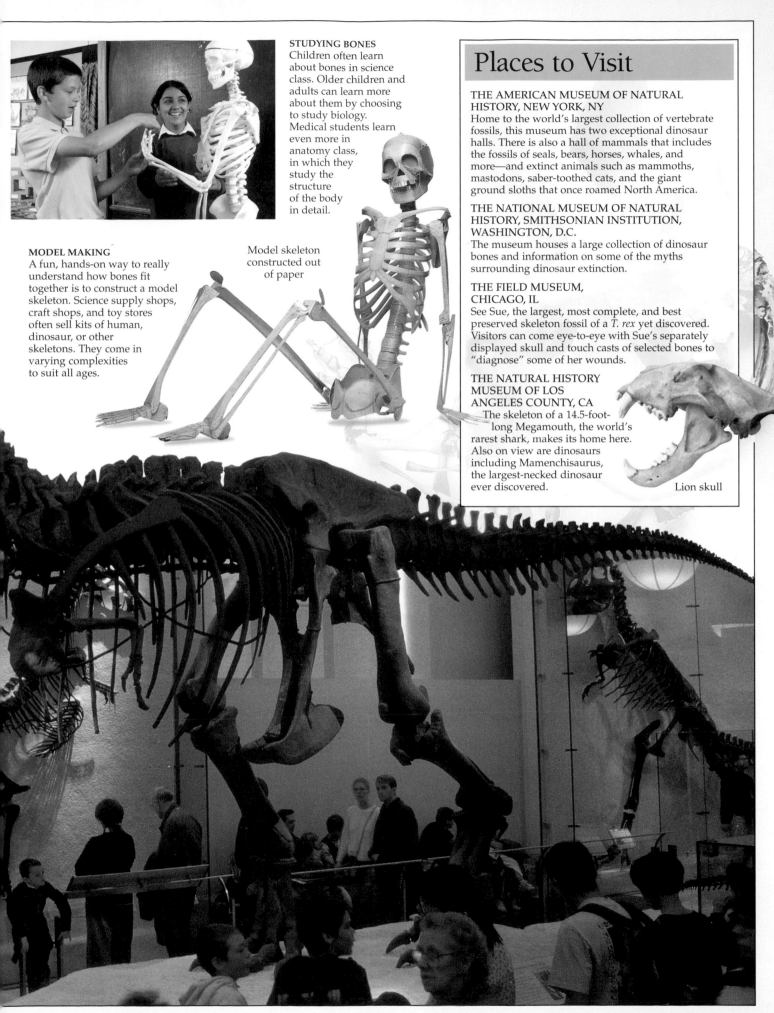

Glossary

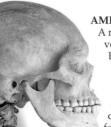

Human backbone

AMPHIBIAN
A member of a class of vertebrates that live both on land and in water, such as a frog

ARACHNID
A member of a class of arthropods with four pairs of legs, such as a spider or a scorpion

ARTHROPOD
A member of the arthropoda division of the animal kingdom. They have a segmented exoskeleton with jointed legs. Arachnids, insects, crustacea, millipedes, and centipedes are all examples of arthropods.

BACKBONE
A strong, flexible chain of bones that runs the length of the body in humans and many other animals. It is also known as the spine or vertebral column.

BONE
A hard body tissue that gives strength to the skeleton. In humans and many animals, it is composed of outer compact bone and inner spongy bone and bone marrow.

CANINE TOOTH
A pointed tooth, usually next to the incisors, that grips and pierces food

CARNASSIAL TOOTH
A specialized tooth on a carnivore that is adapted for tearing meat. Most carnassial teeth are large and long.

CARNIVORE
An animal that eats mainly meat

CARPAL
Vertebrate wrist bone

Hand x-rays showing the replacement of cartilage with bone as a person grows

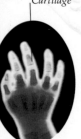
Cartilage

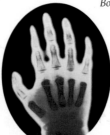

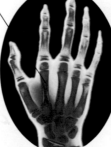
Bone

CARTILAGE
A tough, flexible substance that protects vertebrate joints. It is sometimes called gristle. Cartilaginous fish, such as sharks, have a skeleton made entirely of cartilage.

CHITIN
A light, strong substance found in the exoskeletons of arthropods

COLLAGEN
A connective protein that forms strong, elastic fibers. It is found found in bone and skin.

COMPACT BONE
The hard material that forms the outer layer of a bone

CRANIUM
The part of the skull that surrounds the brain

CRUSTACEAN
A member of a class of mainly aquatic arthropods, such as crab or lobster, with a hard case, or "crust," that encloses the body

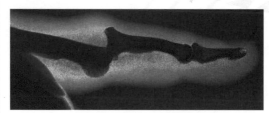
A dislocated finger bone

DENTINE
A hard substance beneath the enamel of vertebrate teeth. It is also known as ivory.

DISLOCATE
A movement that pulls or pushes a bone out of its place within a joint.

ECHINODERM
A marine invertebrate, such as a starfish, with a skeleton made up of hard, bony plates called ossicles

ENAMEL
A tough substance that forms the outer coating of vertebrate teeth

ENDOSKELETON
A hard skeleton found inside an animal's body

EXOSKELETON
A hard skeleton outside of an animal's body

FEMUR
Vertebrate thigh bone

FONTANEL
An area of cartilage in a baby's skull. It turns to bone as the baby grows.

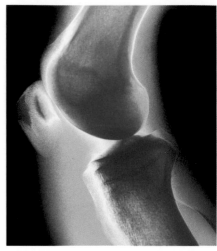
Artificially colored x-ray of knee joint

FORENSIC SCIENCE
The analysis of skeletal or other material in regard to questions of civil or criminal law

GEOLOGY
The science of the Earth's physical history and development

HERBIVORE
An animal that eats mainly plants

HYDROSTATIC SKELETON
An invertebrate skeleton maintained by the internal pressure of the body fluids

INCISOR
A chisel-shaped cutting tooth at the front of the mouth in vertebrates

INVERTEBRATE
An animal that does not have a backbone

JOINT
Any part of a skeleton where two or more bones meet

KERATIN
A structural protein that forms strong, flexible fibers, and makes up horn, hair, and nails

KNUCKLE
A joint between the bones in a finger or thumb

LIGAMENT
A strong, fibrous band of tissue that joins bones together at joints

MANDIBLE
A vertebrate's lower jaw, or the biting mouthpart of an arthropod

MARROW
A substance found within spongy bone. It is where blood cells are made.

MAXILLA
Vertebrate upper jaw, or arthropod mouthpart to rear of the mandible

MOLAR TOOTH
Chewing tooth at the back of a vertebrate jaw

MOLLUSK
An invertebrate with a soft body that is usually covered by a hard shell. The group includes snails, oysters, and scallops.

MOLT
The periodic shedding of an outer covering, such as an exoskeleton, fur, or feathers, to allow for growth or seasonal change

MUMMIFICATION
The process of drying and preserving either human or animal remains by natural or artificial means

NOCTURNAL
Active at night

OMNIVORE
An animal that eats both plant and other animal material

OPPOSABLE
An opposable thumb (in humans) or big toes (in chimps and some other animals) is one that can be manipulated to touch, or oppose, the other fingers or toes on the same hand or foot. This enables the limb to be used for holding and manipulating objects.

ORBIT
A bony socket in which the eyeball is situated

OSSICLE
Any small bone or other calcified structure, such as a plate in an echinoderm shell or an exoskeleton. In humans, it is used to refer to small bones within the ear.

OSSIFICATION
The process whereby cartilage turns into hard bone. In humans, some ossification continues to occur after birth.

PERIOSTEUM
A thin, strong membrane that covers the surface of bones, except at the joints

PHALANGES
The bones of the fingers or toes in vertebrates, including humans

PREMOLAR
Vertebrate tooth that is situated in front of the molars

PRONOTUM
Protective head shield in some insect exoskeletons

REPTILE
A member of a class of vertebrates with scaly skin that lays sealed eggs. Snakes, lizards, and crocodiles are all reptiles.

RODENT
A member of an order of mammals with continuously growing incisors that are kept the right size by continuous gnawing. Rabbits and guinea pigs are both rodents.

SCAPULA
Vertebrate shoulder blade

SEDIMENT
Mineral or organic matter carried and deposited by water, wind, or ice

SEDIMENTARY ROCK
Rock formed from layers of sediment

SINUS
An air-filled hole in the skull. The sinuses around the nasal passages are filled with mucous-producing membranes.

SKELETON
A strong framework that supports the body and, in humans and some animals, provides attachment points for the muscles

SPINAL CORD
The cord of nerve tissue enclosed and protected by the spinal column (backbone). These nerves connect the brain to the rest of the body.

SPONGY BONE
A honeycomblike material in the interior of bones. It is filled with bone marrow.

STERNUM
Vertebrate breast bone

SUTURE
An immovable joint between the individual bones in the skull that helps provide a strong protective casing

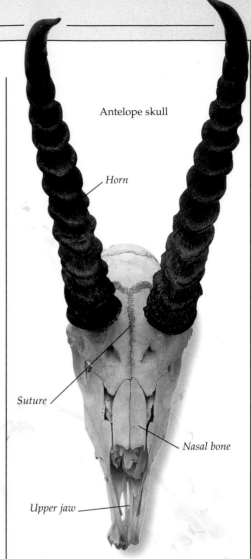

Antelope skull

Horn

Suture

Nasal bone

Upper jaw

TUSK
A vertebrate tooth that projects beyond the upper or lower jaw

VERTEBRA
One of the bones make up the spinal column (backbone)

VERTEBRATE
An animal with a bony or cartilaginous spinal column (backbone)

Image of a human scapula

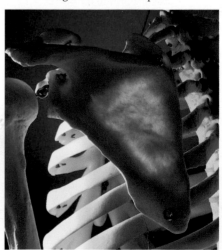

Flexible caudal (tail) fin

Pectoral fin

Vertebra

Cartilaginous dogfish skeleton

Index

Acknowledgments

The publisher would like to thank:

The Booth Museum of Natural History, Brighton, Peter Gardiner, Griffin and George, The Royal College of Surgeons of England, The Royal Veterinary College, and Paul Vos for skeletal material.

Dr. A.V. Mitchell for the x-rays.

Richard and Hilary Bird for the index.

Fred Ford and Mike Pilley of Radius Graphics, and Ray Owen and Nick Madren for artwork.

Anne-Marie Bulat for her work on the initial stages of the book.

Dave King for special photography on pages 14–20 and pages 32–3.

Picture credits
The publisher would like to thank the following for their kind permission to reproduce their images:

Position key: m=middle; b=bottom; l=left; r=right; t=top
American Museum of Natural History: 64tr.
Des and Jen Bartlett/Bruce Coleman Ltd: 51tl
Des and Jen Bartlett/Survival Anglia: 57b
Erwin and Peggy Baurer/Bruce Colema Ltd: 47t
BPCC/Aldus Archive: 9b, 10t, mr, br; 11t; 29b
Booth Museum of Natural History: 68 background
Bridgeman Art Library: 8m; 9ml, 10ml; 11ml
Jane Burton/Bruce Coleman Ltd, 33m
A. Campbell/NHPA: 34b
CNRI/Science Photo Library: 26m; 49tr; 55br; 60tl
Bruce Coleman Ltd: 51br 67br.
A. Davies/NHPA: 34t
Elsdint/Science Photo Library: 60tl
Francisco Eriza/Bruce Coleman Ltd: 50b
FLPA - Images of nature:
Mark Newman 68-9b.
Jeff Foott/Survival Anglia: 50mr, 42m, 48m; 54m
John Freeman, London: 6bl; 7t;

Tom and Pam Gardener/Frank Lane Picture Agency: 33t
P. Boycolea/Alan Hutchinson Library: 11bl
Sonia Halliday Photographs: 43b
E. Hanumantha Rao/NHPA: 53b
Julian Hector/Planet Earth Pictures: 50t
T. Henshaw/Daily Telegraph Colour Library: 54br
Michael Holford: 9t; 11mr; 36t
Eric Hosking: 33br; 51bl; 42tr; 56m
F Jack Jackson/Planet Earth Pictures: 4l
Antony Joyce/Planet Earth Pictures, 33br
Gordon Langsbury/Bruce Coleman Ltd: 32tr
Michael Leach/NHPA: 56t
Mike Linley: 66tl
Lacz Lemoine/NHPA: 32mr
Mansell Collection: 6m; 7m; 15t; 36m; 43t; 56mr; 58t; 61br
Marineland/Frank Lane Picture Agency: 51m
Mary Evans Picture Libvrary: 6tl; br; 7b; 8t, b; 9mr; 10bl; 11br; 13br; 14l, r; 16ml; 26t; 45br; 58ml, mr; 62tl
Masterfile UK: 68bl; Dale Sanders 65cl.
Frieder Michler/Science Photo Library: 60m
Geoff Moon/Frank Lane Picture Agency: 32br
Alfred Pasieka/Bruce Coleman Ltd: 22t
Philip Perry/Frank Lane Picture Agency: 35t
The Natural History Museum, London: 66-7b, 68tr.
Oxford Scientific Films: Harold Taylor 66tr;
M.A. Chappell 67tr.
Education Photos: 69tl.

Dieter and Mary Plage/Bruce Coleman Ltd: 40b
Hans Reinhard/Bruce Coleman Ltd: 32bl; 46bl
Leonard Lee Rue/Bruce Coleman Ltd: 32ml, 52ml
Keith Scholey/Planet Earth Pictures: 50ml
Johnathan Scott/Planet Earth Pictures: 37bl
Silvestris/Frank Lane Picture Agency: 35b
Syndication International: 61bl
Science Photo Library:
68c, 70tr, 70c, 70bl; 71br.
Terry Whittaker/Frank Lane Picture Agency: 52bl
ZEFA: 37t; 39tl; 60b
Gunter Ziesler/Bruce Coleman Ltd: 37 br

Jacket images: Front: Corbis, b.

Illustrations by Will Giles: 12b; 13t, m; 27l, r; 28b; 29t, 34bl, m; 35tl, br; 37m; 38b, 39l, 52b; 44bl, bm, br; 45bl, bm; 46ml, mr, b; 47ml, mr, bl, br, 48ml, 49m; 51tr, 52m, b; 53t, ml, mr; 54bm; 55m; 56t; 59tm

Picture research by: Millie Trowbridge

All other images © Dorling Kindersley.
For further information see:
www.dkimages.com

To Sophia and Nathaniel —K.O.

To Tara —B.R.

Peg and the Yeti
Text © 2004 by Firewing Productions Inc.
Illustrations © 2004 by Barbara Reid
All rights reserved

Published by HarperCollins Publishers Ltd

No part of this book may be used or reproduced in any
manner whatsoever without the prior written permission
of the publisher, except in the case of brief quotations
embodied in reviews.

First Edition

HarperCollins books may be purchased for educational,
business, or sales promotional use through our Special
Markets Department.

HarperCollins Publishers Ltd
2 Bloor Street East, 20th Floor
Toronto, Ontario, Canada
M4W 1A8

www.harpercollins.ca

Library and Archives Canada Cataloguing in Publication

Oppel, Kenneth
Peg and the yeti / by Kenneth Oppel, Barbara Reid. –
1st ed.

ISBN 0-00-200538-7

1. Reid, Barbara, 1957–   II. Title.

PS8579.P64P433 2004   jC813'.54   C2004-903336-0

DWF 9 8 7 6 5 4 3 2 1

Printed and bound in Canada
Set in Caslon Semibold
Photography by Ian Crysler

Peg
AND THE
Yeti

Kenneth Oppel

Barbara Reid

HarperCollinsPublishersLtd

Peg was born upon the bright blue sea.
    Her home was her parents' fishing boat, and
by the time she was eight she'd caught pretty much
every fish that swam. She caught a whale once, but
let it go because a whale is not a fish.

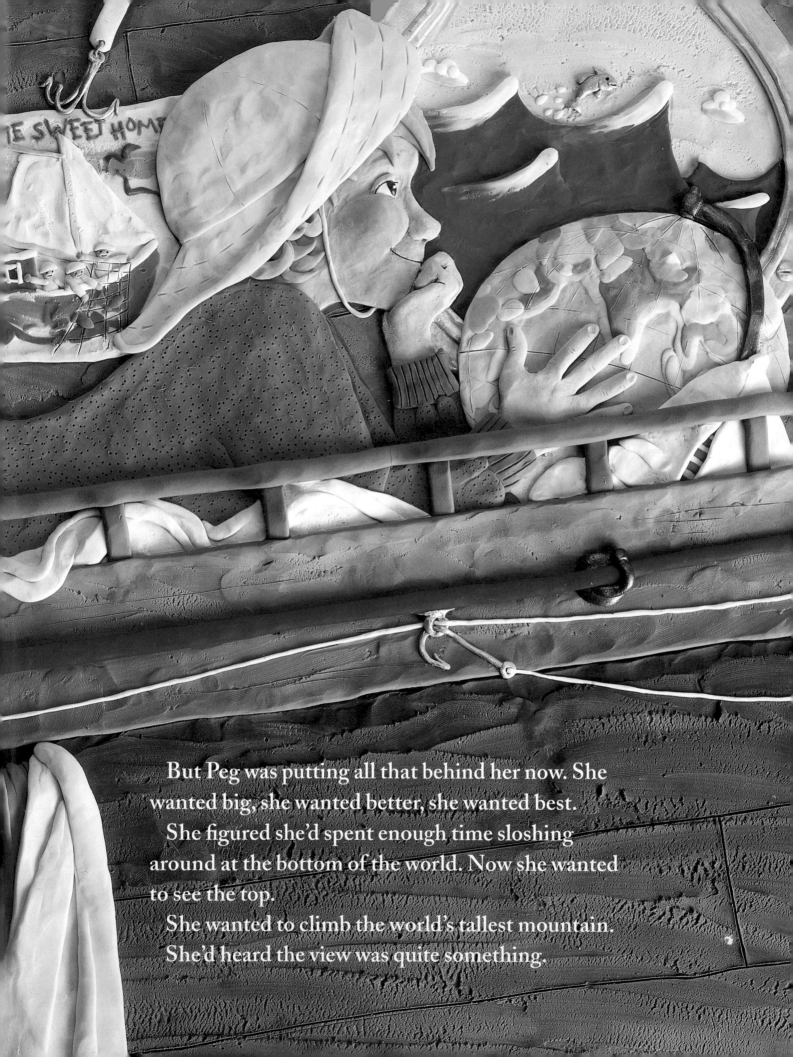

But Peg was putting all that behind her now. She
wanted big, she wanted better, she wanted best.
    She figured she'd spent enough time sloshing
around at the bottom of the world. Now she wanted
to see the top.
    She wanted to climb the world's tallest mountain.
She'd heard the view was quite something.

Peg packed up her fishing rod and said goodbye to her mother and father. She travelled by stagecoach and steamer, rickshaw and water buffalo, and in no time at all, she was at the base of Mount Everest. It stuck right up through the clouds and kept going on the other side.

"Doesn't look so tall to me," Peg said. "But if that's the best there is, I'll just have to put up with it."

After an hour or two, she passed a team of other climbers.

"What d'you think you're doing, lass?" they called after her.

"Climbing the world's tallest mountain," said Peg.

"But you've got no gear!" they exclaimed. "You'll need clamps and cleats and cables! You'll need poles and picks and pulleys! There's wind storms! Avalanches! And they say there's a monster up there — the Yeti!"

"Well, I should hope so," said Peg. "I've been
wanting to see a Yeti."
And up she went.

Peg scaled precipices, skated glaciers, and crossed chasms on icicle ladders. The air moaned, the mountain groaned, and Peg's breath froze solid and clattered to the ground.

"Suppose I better put my mitts on," she said. "It's getting a touch chilly."

Well, a wind came howling down on Peg and tried to blow her halfway to China. Peg was delighted. She rigged herself a sail from her tent and went tacking on up the mountain.

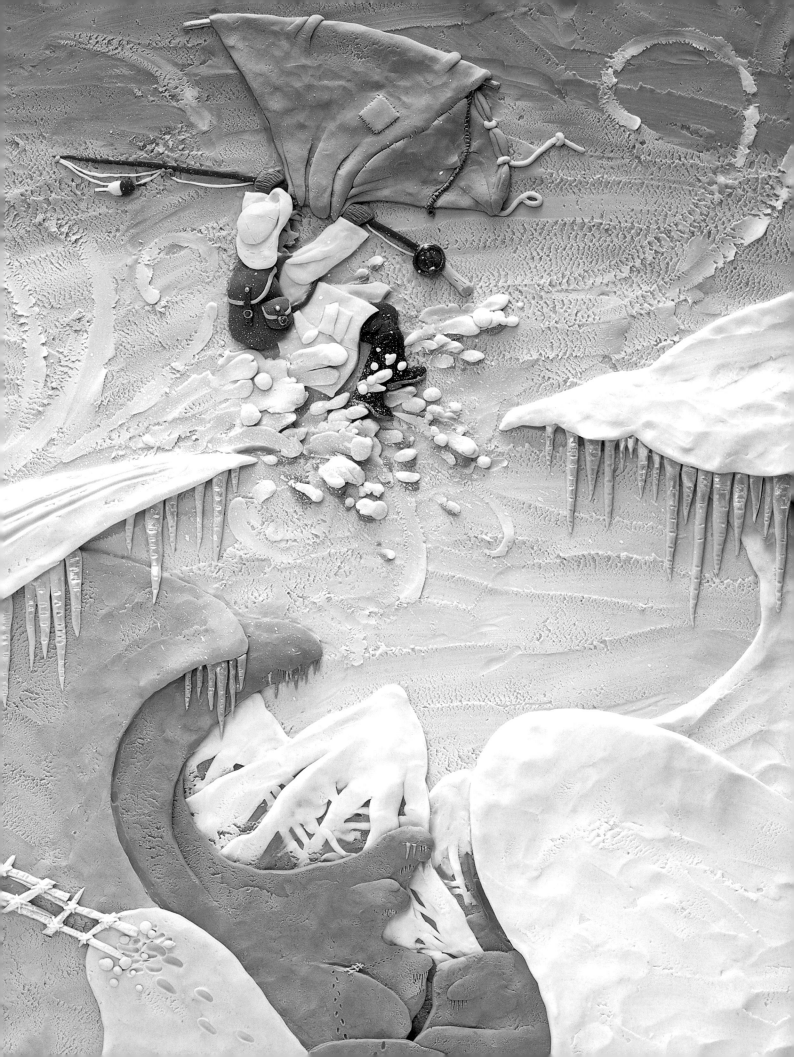

Peg found a cave to spend the night.

She sat down on a big boulder. It was quite soft. It was quite warm. Then she realized she was sitting on the Yeti!

"Poor fellow seems to be having trouble waking up," Peg said. She lifted a paw, spotted an ear, and shouted, "Hey there, Yeti! Wake up!"

The Yeti woke up. He stood up, big as an iceberg, and gave a roar that blasted Peg right out the cave and down the hill. Peg dusted herself off.

The Yeti still seemed a bit out of sorts. He roared again, jumped up and down, banged his fists against the mountain, and started an avalanche that came plunging down towards Peg like a tidal wave.

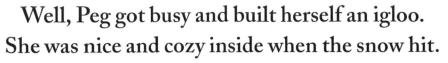

Well, Peg got busy and built herself an igloo.
She was nice and cozy inside when the snow hit.
   Peg made tea. She ate an apple, nibbled some
salted cod, and crunched some pork scruncheons.
Then she wrapped herself up in her blanket and
went to sleep.

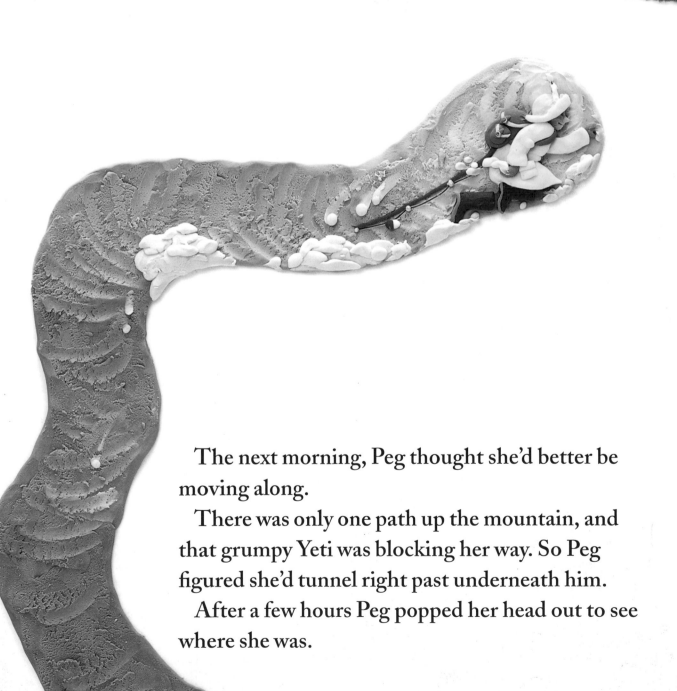

   The next morning, Peg thought she'd better be
moving along.
   There was only one path up the mountain, and
that grumpy Yeti was blocking her way. So Peg
figured she'd tunnel right past underneath him.
   After a few hours Peg popped her head out to see
where she was.

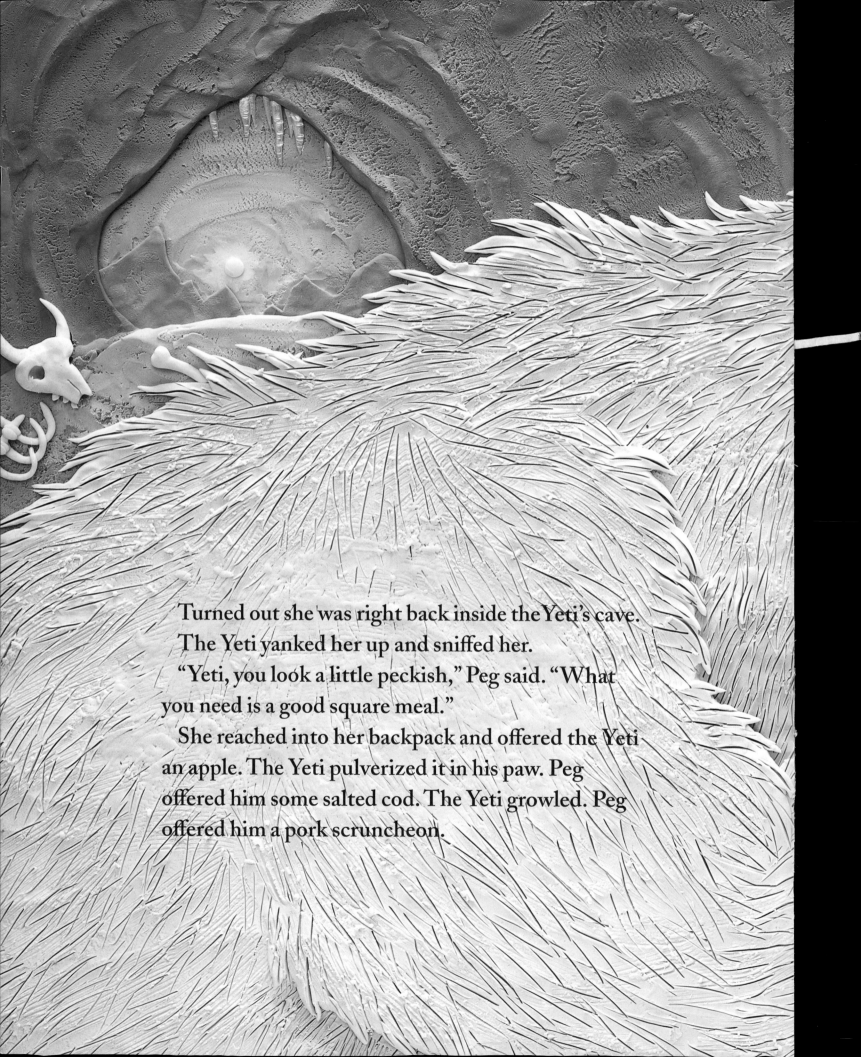

Turned out she was right back inside the Yeti's cave.
The Yeti yanked her up and sniffed her.

"Yeti, you look a little peckish," Peg said. "What you need is a good square meal."

She reached into her backpack and offered the Yeti an apple. The Yeti pulverized it in his paw. Peg offered him some salted cod. The Yeti growled. Peg offered him a pork scruncheon.

The Yeti sniffed it. The Yeti licked it. The Yeti ate it.
He purred and put out his paw for another.
It was a good thing Peg had brought plenty.

Now, Peg reckoned she'd better get going while she and the Yeti were still on friendly terms. The Yeti followed her.

"Go on now, Yeti," Peg said. "I've got a mountain to climb. Shoo, now. Shoo."

But the Yeti would not shoo. He would not go away. He patted her on the shoulder with his big hairy paw. He wanted more scruncheons.

Peg had never met a Yeti so keen on scruncheons.

Up Peg went, towards the clouds.
   But when she got there, they were frozen solid.
She started chipping away with an icicle. The Yeti
covered Peg's ears with his paws and gave a roar so
loud, he shattered the clouds into snowflakes.
   There was the peak!

The Yeti hefted Peg onto his shoulders. He was
a bit shaggy and smelly, but Peg supposed she was a
bit shaggy and smelly by now, too.
In no time at all, they were at the top.

But it wasn't quite the top.

There was one last peak, a needle of sheer ice, high as a lighthouse. Well, Peg wasn't putting up with that.

She got out her fishing rod.

She swung that rod back over her shoulder and cast with all her might. The line played out, higher and higher, and the hook sank into the icy peak.

Peg reeled herself up and stood looking over
the top of the world.
The view was fine.

Peg felt mighty pleased with herself. She'd wanted
to climb the world's tallest mountain, and here she'd
gone and done it—with a little help from the Yeti.

Well, after a few minutes she reckoned it was time to be heading down. But walking seemed just a tad boring now.

Peg got to work. She carved herself a gondola out of ice, started a fire, and filled up her tent like a hot air balloon.

"Goodbye, Yeti," she said. She dumped the last of the scruncheons into his big hairy paw. "Sorry for waking you up. And thanks for your help."

The Yeti climbed aboard with her.

"Go on, Yeti," Peg said. "Shoo, now. Shoo."

But the Yeti would not shoo. He wanted to come too.

"You're too heavy, Yeti!" Peg said. "We'll go nowhere like this."

The Yeti opened her backpack and dumped out the rest of the salted cod.

Slowly, the balloon rose into the air.

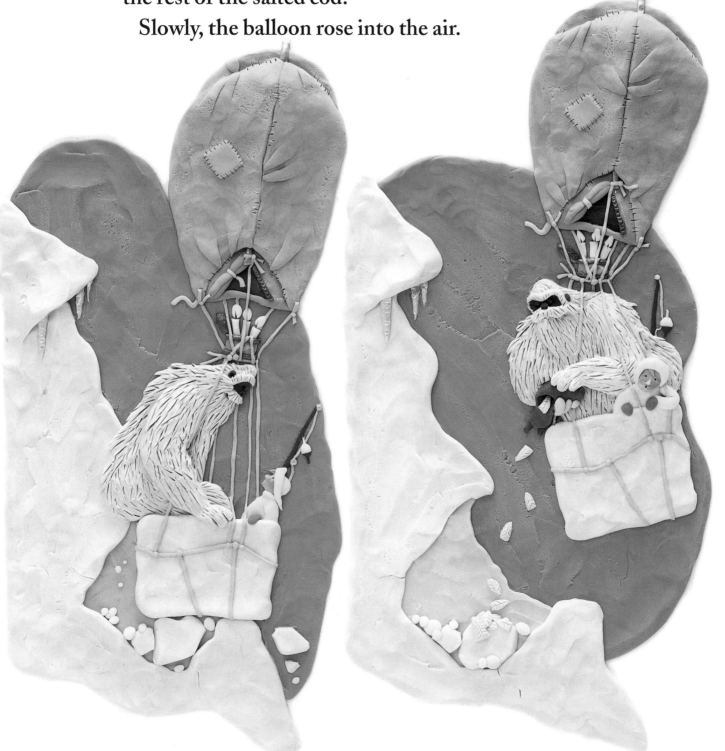

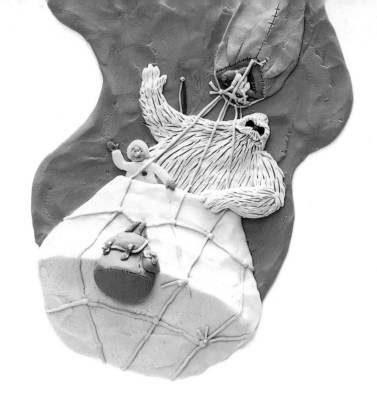

They floated down through the night, the stars close enough to pluck right out of the sky. It was some cold, but Peg and the Yeti curled up together to keep warm.

Next morning, Peg spotted the other climbers.

"Forget the gear!" Peg cried out to them. "Get a Yeti!"

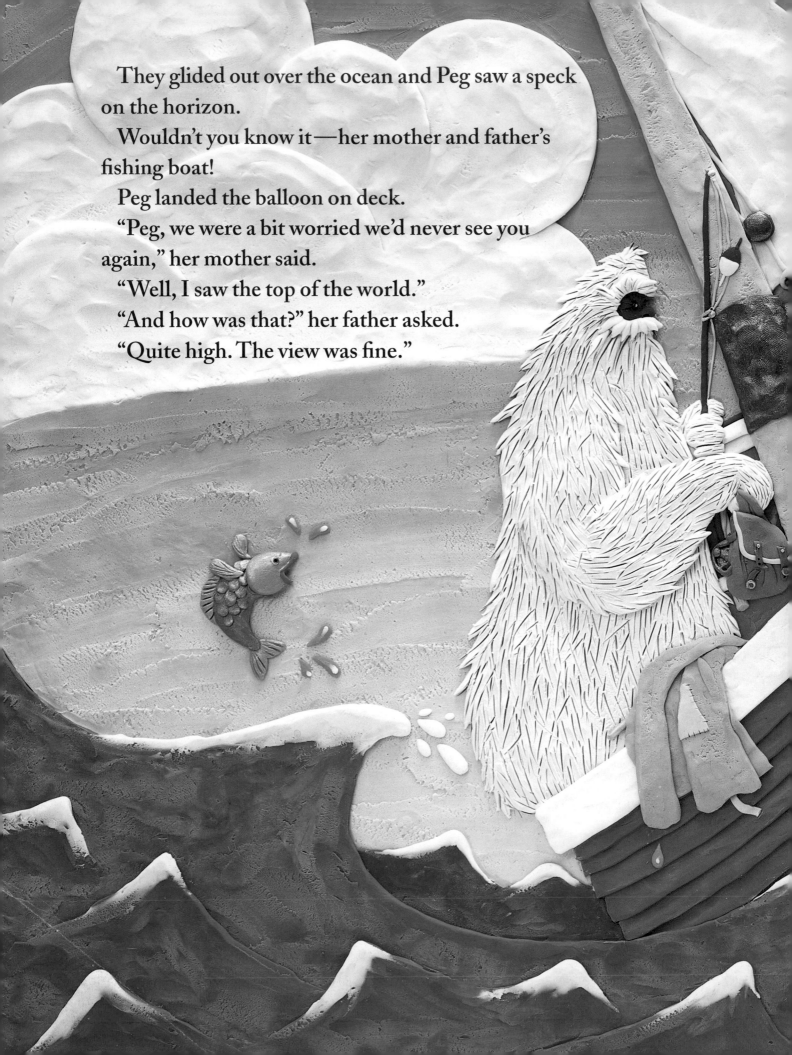

They glided out over the ocean and Peg saw a speck
on the horizon.

Wouldn't you know it—her mother and father's
fishing boat!

Peg landed the balloon on deck.

"Peg, we were a bit worried we'd never see you
again," her mother said.

"Well, I saw the top of the world."

"And how was that?" her father asked.

"Quite high. The view was fine."

"I see you've brought the Yeti with you," her mother said.

"He likes the scruncheons," Peg explained.

"Very good then," said her father.

Well, that Yeti, he took to the sea like nothing else. By the time they reached harbour, he knew how to pull lines, haul sheets and gut fish along with the best of them. He decided to stay on fishing.

But Peg was the restless sort. She was pushing nine, and she figured it was high time she made something of her life. After all, she wanted big, she wanted better, she wanted best.

And she'd already set her sights on something new.

APATOSAURUS

AND OTHER GIANT, LONG-NECKED PLANT-EATERS

Prehistoric World

APATOSAURUS

AND OTHER GIANT, LONG-NECKED PLANT-EATERS

VIRGINIA
SCHOMP

Benchmark Books

MARSHALL CAVENDISH
NEW YORK

DINOSAURS LIVED MILLIONS OF YEARS AGO. EVERYTHING WE KNOW ABOUT THEM—HOW THEY LOOKED, WALKED, ATE, FOUGHT, MATED, AND RAISED THEIR YOUNG—COMES FROM EDUCATED GUESSES BY THE SCIENTISTS WHO DISCOVER AND STUDY FOSSILS. THE INFORMATION IN THIS BOOK IS BASED ON WHAT MOST SCIENTISTS BELIEVE RIGHT NOW. TOMORROW OR NEXT WEEK OR NEXT YEAR, NEW DISCOVERIES COULD LEAD TO NEW IDEAS. SO KEEP YOUR EYES AND EARS OPEN FOR NEWS FLASHES FROM THE PREHISTORIC WORLD!

With thanks to Dr. Mark A. Norell, Chairman of the Division of Paleontology, American Museum of Natural History, for his expert review of the manuscript.

Benchmark Books
Marshall Cavendish
99 White Plains Road
Tarrytown, New York 10591-9001
www.marshallcavendish.com

Library of Congress Cataloging-in-Publication Data

Schomp, Virginia.
Apatosaurus and other giant long-necked plant-eaters / by Virginia Schomp
    p. cm. (Prehistoric World)
Includes index and bibliographical references.
Summary: Discusses the traits and habits of Apatosaurus and other giant long-necked plant-eaters.
ISBN 0-7614-1022-8
1. Apatosaurus—Juvenile literature. 2. Herbivores, Fossil—Juvenile literature. 3. Dinosaurs—Juvenile literature.
[1. Apatosaurus. 2. Herbivores, Fossil. 3. Dinosaurs.] I. Title.
QE862.S3 S32 2002   567.913-dc21   2001043988

Front cover: *Apatosaurus*   Back cover: *Omeisaurus*   Pages 2–3: *Diplodocus*

Photo Credits:
Cover illustration: The Natural History Museum, London / John Sibbick

The illustrations and photographs in this book are used by the permission and through the courtesy of:
Corbis: Bob Krist, 12. *Marshall Cavendish Corporation:* 2-3, 8, 9, 10, 11, 13, 16-17, 18, 19, 20, 21, 22, 23, 24, 25, back cover.

Map and Dinosaur Family Tree by Robert Romagnoli

Printed in Hong Kong
1 3 5 6 4 2

For Tommy, Kenny, and Danny

Contents

EARTH'S REAL-LIFE GIANTS

A small mouselike creature nibbles on seeds in an ancient evergreen grove. Suddenly the earth shakes. A gigantic dinosaur looms overhead, its long neck stretching to the top of the trees. As the tiny mammal dives for shelter, the rest of the giant's herd thunder near, smashing their way through the woods. Opening their jaws wide, the hungry dinosaurs start to feast. They gulp down tons of leaves and twigs. Then they move on, leaving a trail of trampled earth and bare branches.

BRACHIOSAURUS
(brack-ee-oh-SORE-us)
When: Late Jurassic,
  155–145 million years ago
Where: Colorado and
  East Africa
◆ **Heavier than 6 to 7 large**
  elephants
◆ **Huge nostrils on top of head**

Brachiosaurus, *a cousin of* Apatosaurus, *filled its giant-sized stomach with hundreds of pounds of vegetation each day.*

As long as two city buses. Taller than a two-story house. It's hard to imagine a creature as big as *Apatosaurus*. This awesome giant belonged to the sauropods—a group of dinosaurs that included the largest land animals the world has ever known. The chart on page 26 shows how *Apatosaurus* and the other skyscraping sauropods fit into the dinosaur family tree.

All sauropods were plant-eaters. They had extra-long necks, huge bodies, and long tails. The "smallest" of these giants was thirty feet long. The largest may have stretched twice as long as a bowling alley and weighed one hundred tons—more than a fully loaded tractor trailer.

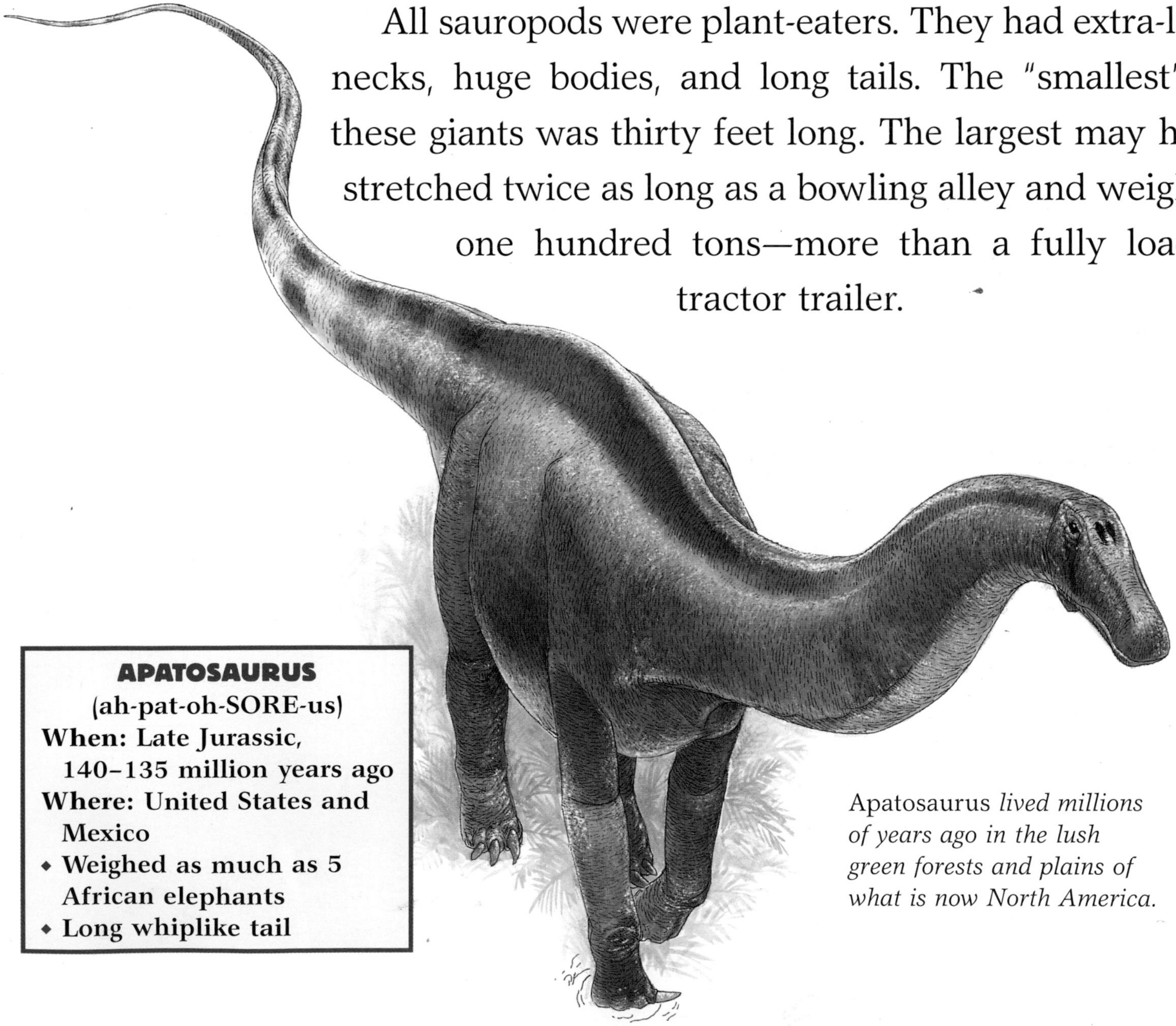

APATOSAURUS
(ah-pat-oh-SORE-us)
When: Late Jurassic,
   140–135 million years ago
Where: United States and
   Mexico
• **Weighed as much as 5
   African elephants**
• **Long whiplike tail**

Apatosaurus *lived millions of years ago in the lush green forests and plains of what is now North America.*

COLOSSAL COUSINS

Imagine five large elephants all rolled into one enormous animal. *Apatosaurus* carried all that weight on four massive legs ending in broad, elephant-like feet. When it walked, this giant plant-eater held its long tail off the ground. Its hoselike neck swung gently from side to side, searching for tasty greens. Like all sauropods, *Apatosaurus* had a small head. Lots of skinny, pencil-like teeth crowded the front of its mouth. Its brain was 100,000 times lighter than its body and not much bigger than a golf ball.

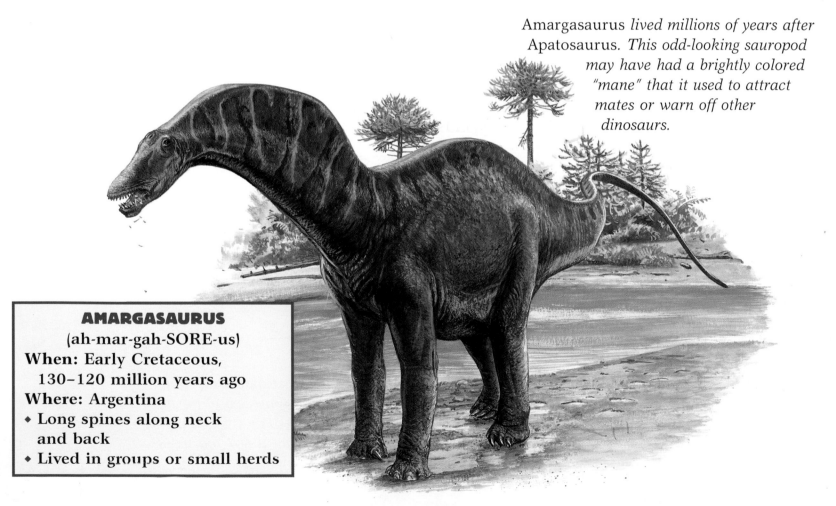

Amargasaurus *lived millions of years after* Apatosaurus. *This odd-looking sauropod may have had a brightly colored "mane" that it used to attract mates or warn off other dinosaurs.*

AMARGASAURUS
(ah-mar-gah-SORE-us)
When: Early Cretaceous,
130–120 million years ago
Where: Argentina
- Long spines along neck and back
- Lived in groups or small herds

Apatosaurus is the most famous sauropod, but it had many cousins. *Amargasaurus* had high backbone spines that looked something like a horse's mane. *Mamenchisaurus* had the longest neck of any dinosaur—50 feet, or more than half its body length.

MAMENCHISAURUS
(mah-men-chee-SORE-us)
When: Middle Jurassic,
160 million years ago
Where: China
♦ Neck longer than a bus
♦ Largest dinosaur ever
found in Asia

Long-necked Mamenchisaurus *could stand in one place and feed from the tallest treetops or gobble up all the low-growing plants in a large field*

BYE-BYE, *BRONTOSAURUS*

You may know *Apatosaurus* by another name. In the 1870s Othniel Charles Marsh, a famous American paleontologist (a scientist who studies prehistoric life), discovered two new dinosaur skeletons. He named one *Apatosaurus* and the other *Brontosaurus*. Nearly a century later, scientists realized that the two were really the same animal. Because *Apatosaurus* was the first name given to this dinosaur, that's what it is officially called today.

Paleontologists learn about prehistoric life by studying fossils. Some of their discoveries, like this skeleton of the sauropod Barosaurus, *may be displayed in museums.*

DINOSAUR DAYS

Dinosaurs walked the earth for a very long time—about 165 million years. Scientists divide the Age of Dinosaurs into three parts. *Apatosaurus* and many other giant sauropods lived during the second part, the Jurassic period, from 205 million to 135 million years ago.

CETIOSAURUS
(see-tee-oh-SORE-us)
When: Early to Middle Jurassic,
180–170 million years ago
Where: North Africa and England
◆ As long as a great whale
◆ Thighbones as tall as a man

The first sauropod ever discovered, Cetiosaurus had "old-fashioned" features such as a heavy, solid backbone, instead of the lighter, hollowed-out backbone of many later sauropods.

The world looked very different in Jurassic times. At the beginning of the period, all the continents were joined together in one huge landmass, surrounded by sea. Over the centuries, earthquakes shook the earth and volcanoes exploded. The supercontinent slowly split into two large land-masses: Laurasia in the north and Gondwanaland in the south.

PLANT-EATERS' PARADISE

Let's take a trip back in time 140 million years, to the Late Jurassic period. The air feels warm and sticky here. Breezes from the spreading seas carry rain far inland, turning even the deserts green. Lush forests of evergreens, fruit-bearing ginkgo trees, and towering tree ferns cover the land.

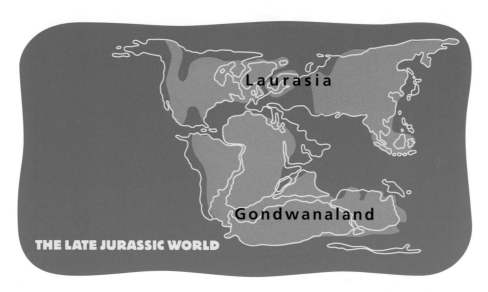

Laurasia and Gondwanaland broke up and drifted apart, to form the continents we know today. The yellow outlines on the map show the shape of the modern continents; the green shading shows their position 140 million years ago.

The Age of Dinosaurs

Dinosaurs walked the earth during the Mesozoic era, also known as the Age of Dinosaurs. The Mesozoic era lasted from about 250 million to 65 million years ago. It is divided into three periods: the Triassic, Jurassic, and Cretaceous.

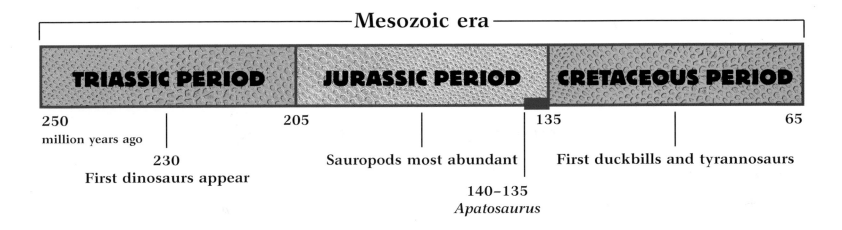

Mesozoic era

TRIASSIC PERIOD | JURASSIC PERIOD | CRETACEOUS PERIOD

250 million years ago

230
First dinosaurs appear

205

Sauropods most abundant

140–135
Apatosaurus

135

First duckbills and tyrannosaurs

65

This salad bar world is a perfect setting for *Apatosaurus* and its plant-eating cousins. These giants live alongside many smaller plant-eaters as well as fierce meat-eating dinosaurs, including sharp-toothed, two-ton *Allosaurus*. Other kinds of animals also share the Jurassic world. There are monstrous sea reptiles, fish, frogs, birds, insects, and small furry mammals. But the undisputed rulers of the land are the dinosaurs. And none of the dinosaurs have a greater impact on the world around them than the big-bellied, always hungry sauropods.

Diplodocus, *which lived in North America at the same time as Apatosaurus, could use its long whiplike tail to fight off this group of fierce meat-eating* Allosaurus.

16

DIPLODOCUS
(dih-PLOH-doh-kus)
When: Late Jurassic,
150–135 million years ago
Where: United States
◆ Longer than a tennis court
◆ Strong but hollow backbone,
for reduced weight

LIFESTYLES OF THE BIG AND HUNGRY

When *Apatosaurus* passed through North America's forests and plains, it was like a natural disaster. This hungry giant spent about eighteen hours a day feeding. A small group of *Apatosaurus* could gulp down several acres of trees in just a few hours.

> **CAMARASAURUS**
> (KAM-uh-ruh-sore-us)
> **When:** Late Jurassic,
> 150–135 million years ago
> **Where:** western United
> States and Portugal
> ◆ Shorter neck than most
> sauropods
> ◆ Strong, spoon-shaped teeth

Because Camarasaurus *dined on low tree branches, it could share the North American feeding grounds of longer-necked relatives such as* Apatosaurus *and* Diplodocus.

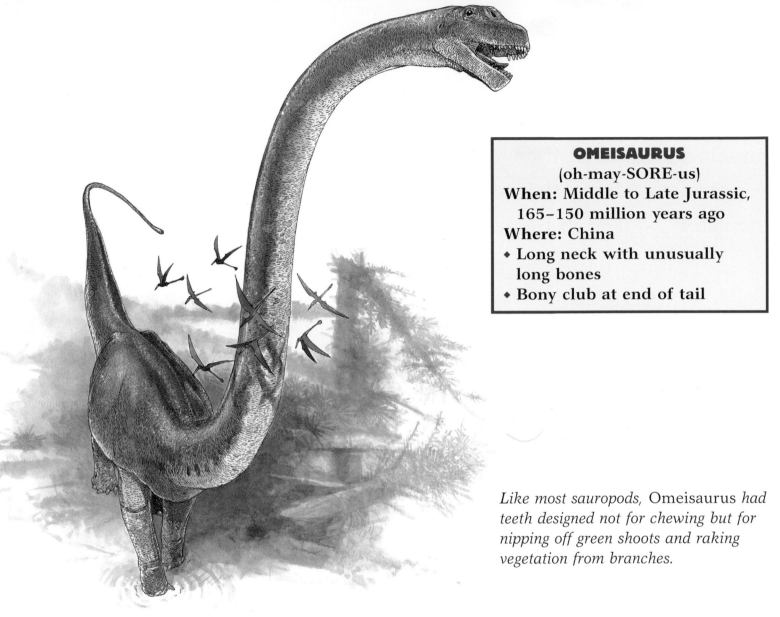

Like most sauropods, Omeisaurus *had teeth designed not for chewing but for nipping off green shoots and raking vegetation from branches.*

"Gulp" is the right word. Sauropods didn't chew their food. Instead, an *Apatosaurus* closed its rakelike teeth over a branch and pulled, stripping off all the leaves, needles, cones, and twigs. Then it swallowed. To digest this difficult diet, sauropods swallowed stones, too. In the dinosaur's huge belly, these "stomach stones," or gastroliths, helped pound tons of tough plant food into pulp.

BRINGING UP BABY

For protection from predators, sauropods may have lived in herds. The animals in the herd traveled together in a constant search for food. As they trudged along, the adults stayed on the outside of the herd. The youngsters walked in the middle, sheltered from harm.

These footprints were made during the Late Jurassic period by a herd of sauropods traveling across what is now Texas. Just like skeletons, footprints left long ago in soft ground can harden into fossils.

Sauropods probably didn't care for their own young. If a herd stayed in one place too long, waiting for eggs to hatch, it would eat up all the food and starve. Besides, hatchlings weren't fast enough to keep up with a traveling herd. So mothers just laid their eggs and moved on. A baby crawling from its shell was on its own. Luckily, a newly hatched *Apatosaurus* may have already measured three feet long, and it knew how to run, hide, and nibble on greens.

Many babies were caught by predators. Many others survived and grew strong. By the time an *Apatosaurus* was five years old, it had probably reached half its adult size. Seeking out other *Apatosaurus*, the young dinosaur was ready to take its place in the shelter of the herd.

This tiny Mussaurus *has just hatched from its egg.* Mussaurus *was probably a prosauropod—an early relative and possible ancestor of the giant sauropods.*

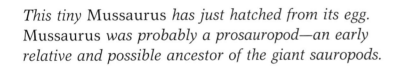

MUSSAURUS
(muh-SORE-us)
When: Late Triassic, 215 million years ago
Where: Argentina
◆ Only baby skeletons have ever been found
◆ 8 inches long (adults may have grown to 10 feet)

FIERCE FIGHTERS

Sauropods were gentle giants, but they weren't defenseless. With a flick of its whiplike tail, the sauropod could knock an attacker to the ground. Stomping down with its massive legs, a twenty-five-ton *Apatosaurus* could trample a menacing meat-eater to death. The sharp claws on its feet may also have served as deadly weapons.

DATOUSAURUS
(dah-toh-SORE-us)
When: Middle Jurassic,
  170 million years ago
Where: China
  ◆ **Bigger head than most**
    sauropods
  ◆ **Spoon-shaped teeth for**
    crushing plants

Datousaurus *may have defended itself by rearing up on its back legs and lashing out with the sharp claws on its front feet.*

SHUNOSAURUS
(shoo-no-SORE-us)
When: Middle Jurassic,
175–163 million years ago
Where: China
- Shorter neck than most
sauropods
- Bony tail club with spikes

Few creatures dared to attack a healthy full-grown sauropod. If it was threatened, this Shunosaurus *had an unusual weapon—a bony tail club for whacking attackers.*

END OF THE GIANTS

At the end of the Jurassic period, *Apatosaurus* and many of its sauropod cousins died out, or became extinct. Paleontologists aren't sure why. Some think that these sauropods couldn't eat the new kinds of flowering plants that began to grow, crowding out the evergreen forests.

Sauropods that lived on included members of the titanosaur family. Titanosaurs were large, long-necked plant-eaters with bony armor. They survived to the end of the Cretaceous period, sixty-five million years ago. Then all the dinosaurs mysteriously disappeared.

TITANOSAURUS
(tie-tah-no-SORE-us)
When: Late Cretaceous,
  80–65 million years ago
Where: Argentina, India,
  France, Madagascar
◆ One of the last
  sauropods
◆ Three times the height
  of a man

Titanosaurus *gave its name to the titanosaurs, a family of large Late Cretaceous sauropods with protective armor.*

After most of the sauropods had died out, Argentinosaurus *was still going strong in the forests of South America. Some paleontologists think that this giant may have been the heaviest animal that ever lived.*

ARGENTINOSAURUS
(ar-jen-teen-oh-SORE-us)
When: Early Cretaceous,
   120–100 million years ago
Where: Argentina
◆ Legs 16 feet long
◆ May have weighed 100 tons

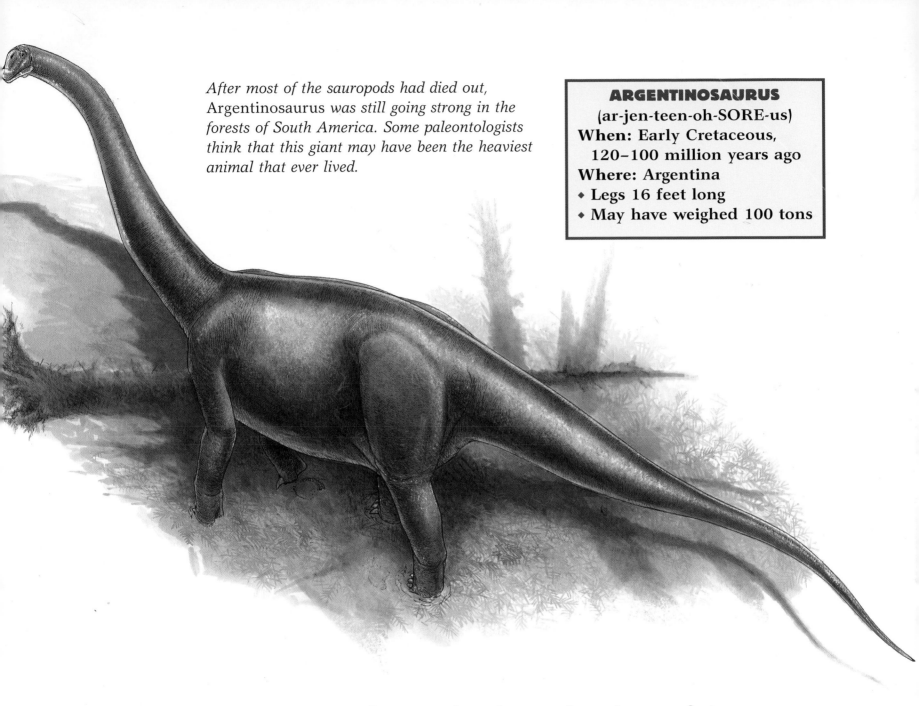

Today no creature comes close to the size and majesty of *Apatosaurus* and the other colossal sauropods. But we are lucky that these amazing animals left behind clues to give us a picture of what life was like when giants walked the earth.

Dinosaur Family Tree

ORDER — All dinosaurs are divided into two large groups, based on the shape and position of their hipbones. Saurischians had forward-pointing hipbones.

SUBORDER — Sauropodomorphs were long-necked plant-eating dinosaurs.

INFRAORDER — Sauropods were the largest land animals that ever lived.

FAMILY — A family includes one or more types of closely related dinosaurs.

GENUS — Every dinosaur has a two-word name. The first word tells us what genus, or type, of dinosaur it is. The genus plus the second word tell us its species—the group of very similar animals it belongs to. (For example, *Apatosaurus ajax* is one species of *Apatosaurus*.)

Scientists organize all living things into groups, according to features shared.
This chart shows the groupings of the giant, long-necked plant-eaters in this book.

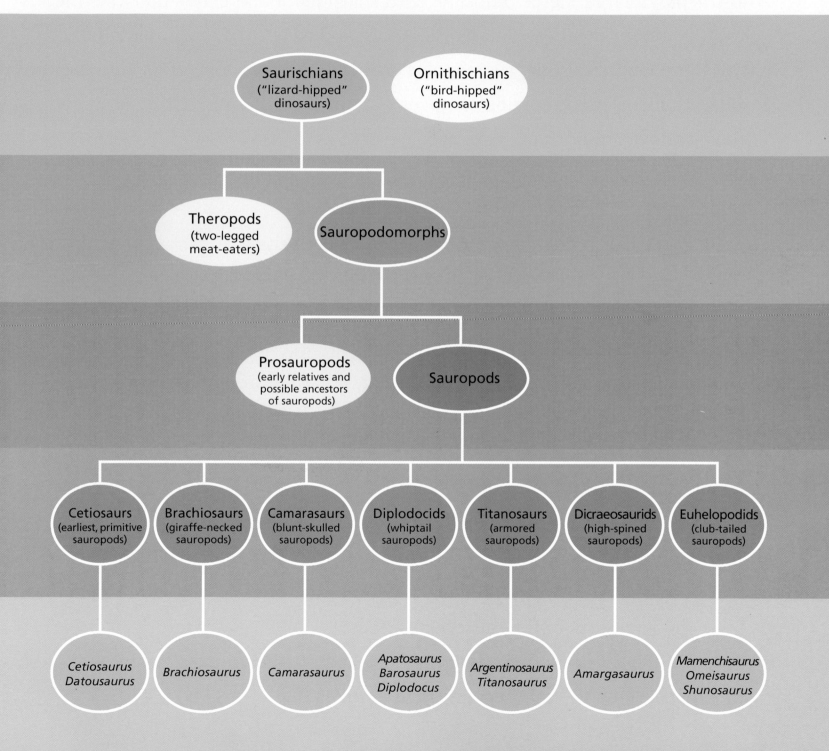

Glossary

Allosaurus: a large, fierce dinosaur with sharp teeth and claws that was the most common meat-eater in North America during the Late Jurassic period

extinct: no longer existing; an animal is extinct when every one of its kind has died

fossils: the hardened remains or traces of animals or plants that lived many thousands or millions of years ago

gastroliths: stones swallowed by many dinosaurs (and modern birds) to help grind up their food

ginkgo: a tree with fan-shaped leaves and silvery nuts that first appeared during the Age of Dinosaurs and still grows today

Jurassic (joo-RA-sick) **period:** the time period from 205 million to 135 million years ago, when *Apatosaurus* and most of the other sauropods lived

mammal: an animal that is warm-blooded, breathes air, and nurses its young with milk; humans are mammals

paleontologist (pay-lee-on-TAH-luh-jist)**:** a scientist who studies fossils to learn about dinosaurs and other forms of prehistoric life

predators: animals that hunt and kill other animals for food

prosauropods (pro-SORE-uh-pods)**:** medium-sized, long-necked, plant-eating dinosaurs that first appeared near the end of the Triassic period and may have been the ancestors of the sauropods

sauropods (SORE-uh-pods)**:** giant, long-necked plant-eating dinosaurs that were the largest, longest, and heaviest land animals that ever lived

Find Out More

BOOKS

Coleman, Graham. *Looking at Apatosaurus/Brontosaurus*. Milwaukee:
Gareth Stevens, 1995.

Dixon, Dougal. *Dougal Dixon's Amazing Dinosaurs: The Fiercest, the Tallest, the Toughest, the Smallest*. Honesdale, PA: Boyds Mills, 2000.

The Humongous Book of Dinosaurs. New York: Stewart, Tabori, and Chang, 1997.

Lindsay, William. *On the Trail of Incredible Dinosaurs*. New York: DK Publishing, 1998.

Marshall, Chris, ed. *Dinosaurs of the World*. 11 vols. New York: Marshall Cavendish, 1999.

Parker, Steve. *The Age of Dinosaurs*. Vol. 4, *The Sauropods*. Danbury, CT: Grolier Educational, 2000.

ON-LINE SOURCES *

Carnegie Museum of Natural History at **http://www.clpgh.org/cmnh**

A giant sauropod greets you as you enter Pittsburgh's Carnegie Museum of Natural History. Click on "exhibits" to visit the Jurassic Classroom of the museum's Dinosaur Hall, featuring a 3-D image of the hall, a fossil slide show, live web cams, and more.

*Website addresses sometimes change. For more on-line sources, check with the media specialist at your local library.

Dinorama **at http://www.nationalgeographic.com/dinorama/frame.html**

Get the latest news on dinosaur discoveries at this National Geographic Society site.

Kinetosaurs **at http://www.childrensmuseum.org/kinetosaur**

Inspired by a traveling museum exhibit of moving dinosaur art, this site spon–sored by the Children's Museum of Indianapolis gives step-by-step instructions for making dinosaur sculptures and other projects. Also includes fact sheets and printouts on *Apatosaurus* and other prehistoric creatures.

University of California, Berkeley, Museum of Paleontology **at http://www.ucmp.berkeley.edu**

Explore the exhibits at the Museum of Paleontology, which include a mounted *Diplodocus,* scenes from Jurassic life, and great children's drawings of dinosaurs.

UW Geological Museum Tour **at http://www.uwyo.edu/geomuseum/Tour.htm**

Tour the University of Wyoming Geological Museum, where exhibits include a seventy-five-foot-long *Apatosaurus* discovered in Wyoming.

Zoom Dinosaurs **at http://www.zoomdinosaurs.com**

This colorful, entertaining site from Enchanted Learning Software includes a world of information on dinosaur-related topics: dinosaur myths, records, behavior, and fossils; dinosaur fact sheets; quizzes, puzzles, printouts, and crafts; tips on writing a school report; and more.

Index

Virginia Schomp grew up in a quiet suburban town in northeastern New Jersey, where eight-ton duck-billed dinosaurs once roamed. In first grade she discovered that she loved books and writing, and in sixth grade she was named "class bookworm," because she always had her nose in a book. Today she is a freelance author who has written more than thirty books for young readers on topics including careers, animals, ancient cultures, and modern history. Ms. Schomp lives in the Catskill Mountain region of New York with her husband, Richard, and their son, Chip.